Poetry Collections by Ruth Naylor

A Family Affair

Straw & All: A Christmas Poetry Collection

FAITH TALK:

a spiritual memoir inviting reflection & dialogue

Ruth Naylor

Ruth Naylor

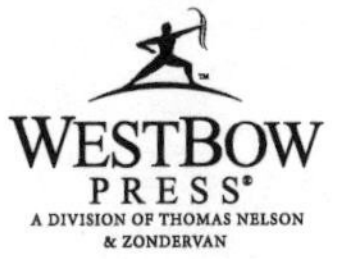

WestBow Press books may be ordered through booksellers or by contacting:

WestBow Press
A Division of Thomas Nelson & Zondervan
1663 Liberty Drive
Bloomington, IN 47403
www.westbowpress.com
1 (866) 928-1240

ISBN: 978-1-9736-6629-5 (sc)
ISBN: 978-1-9736-6631-8 (hc)
ISBN: 978-1-9736-6630-1 (e)

Library of Congress Control Number: 2019908061

Print information available on the last page.

WestBow Press rev. date: 07/30/2019

To my family and friends–former, current, and yet to be.

"Say not, 'I have found the truth,' but rather, 'I have found a truth.'

Say not, 'I have found the path of the soul.'

Say rather, 'I have met the soul walking upon my path.'

For the soul walks upon all paths.

The soul walks not upon a line, neither does it grow like a reed.

The soul unfolds itself, like a lotus of countless petals."

Kahlil Gibran, The Prophet

Contents

Introduction: How to Use This Book

Without being prescriptive, the stories in this spiritual memoir look at life through the eyes of faith. They are intended to encourage readers of all faiths (or of little faith) to reflect upon the presence and providence of God in their own lives, upon their spoken or unspoken prayers, and upon their evolving relationship with God and others. The book encourages deep faith sharing in group settings.

This is not a what-to-believe or how-to-do-it book. It is about how spiritual growth has happened and is still happening in the author's life. These true stories reveal challenges to faith as well as affirmations. The book speaks to those who seek wisdom beyond their own and who would like to know how others interact with the available spiritual power that the author calls the Holy Spirit and God. It is for those who seek to know and trust God personally –with the heart, not just with the mind.

The author's spiritual life has been influenced by a Contemplative Quaker upbringing plus Evangelical, Pentecostal, and Anabaptist influences at different points in her life –all of which have insights to offer. Without being preachy, these stories invite thought and further exploration, affirmation, expansion or disagreement.

The stories are not always in chronological order because each chapter has its own theme and some of them recur at different times in life. Questions at the end of each chapter encourage readers to think about such things as their spiritual roots and how what they believe has shaped their own life-experiences. No two writer or reader life-stories are the same.

Vulnerability can be part of honest sharing such as the author is doing in these pages, but there is challenge and sometimes even healing in sharing stories of faith. An open and respectful atmosphere is required for good group sharing, but there needs to be an understanding about confidentiality where it is desired.

Dealing with just one chapter at a sitting, whether the book is being used for personal or group reflection, will provide better opportunity to focus on the issue(s) at hand before going on. Using the book in a group setting invites a wide sharing of faith and a worthwhile chance to respond to each other.

Preface

I had just completed a three-part sermon series on prayer, which included a number of personal examples, and was standing at the sanctuary door of Grace Mennonite Church (Pandora, Ohio) greeting Sunday morning worshipers. As they shook hands with me, their summer interim pastor, a number of them expressed particular appreciation for my personal sharing. Then they headed on home for dinner, a game of golf, or an afternoon nap.

But one, an elderly member of our local Writers Group, gripped my hand firmly and with an air of spinster authority announced, "Ruth, you must put those sermons into a book." I knew instinctively that I did not want to do a book of sermons. But her admonition echoed somewhere deep within me. It challenged. It encouraged. It said, "Your spiritual development and prayer are things you could and maybe should write about someday."

I am not an authority on anything. What I know for sure about faith is how it has directed my life. Even that is filled with mystery. A number of years ago, I happened to be in conversation about prayer and faith with a pastor who was focused on political action. His parting comment was, "Well, I am not a mystic." Hmmm. It seemed he was implying that I was a mystic, and I wasn't even familiar with that term. His response made me wonder. I looked up the term in a dictionary but still had to wonder if he was right.

More recently Richard Rohr, a well-known Franciscan priest, included the following statement in one of his Internet devotionals: **"Remember that mysticism is simply experiential knowing rather than intellectual knowing."** Having lived three-quarters of my life now in a congregation with many university professors who are committed to intellectual scholarship in the pursuit of Truth, that quotation sheds light on a different but probably equally relevant way of knowing more about God. This book is about knowing God through a lifetime of personal experience. And yes, I now believe that I am a mystic, and in reflecting while writing this book, it has been interesting to see how my faith has evolved.

In my fifties, after hearing and writing years of carefully constructed, well worded prayers, I began to study contemplative prayer. Only then did I realize that I had been in that familiar terrain before –not intellectually, but experientially. Many of my current conversations with God have circled around to being much like what I experienced in the worshipful silence of my Quaker childhood and adolescence where listening for what God has to say to me is fully as important, if not more important, as heartfelt petition.

I began to write this spiritual memoir years ago and shared my beginning chapters with one of the professionals at a Christian Writers Conference. His comment was, "It's obvious that you know how to write. You need to put some questions for reflection and possible discussion at the end of each chapter and then send what you have along with a query letter and a complete chapter outline to potential publishers." I took his advice and sent it to four or five publishers. There were no takers although a couple of them took the time to make some encouraging comments.

Alas, I was discouraged and put the partial manuscript away. Three years ago, two of my adult grandchildren and I were sitting in front of a blazing fire in the family room just chatting while waiting for our family Christmas dinner to be served. They began asking about how faith had impacted my life; so, I shared some of the stories that are now in this book. They paid rapt attention and asked a lot of questions. When the meal was ready, they both were adamant saying, "Gram, you must write these stories down --even if it is just for us."

With their encouragement, I dug out the unfinished manuscript and continued.

In my life, wordless knowing has evolved into a desire for words to describe the personal, mystical, and undefinable! Stories and poems in this memoir are all part of my spiritual life. They are related to my understanding of God, prayer, providence, and guidance whether explicitly stated or not. Words are never perfect.

Where words fall short, perhaps a Higher Wisdom can intervene and make the Presence known. As the Apostle Paul and Timothy wrote to their friends at Philippi:

> ***This is my prayer: that your love might become even more and more rich with knowledge and all kinds of insight. I pray this so that you will be able to decide what really matters . . .***
>
> **–Philippians 1:9-10a, CEB**

Caught in Communication

Experience captured
and put on the page,
no matter how
wonderfully contrived
the words,
is like an untamed animal
caught
and put into a zoo
where others come to look
--even marvel.

Words are a pathetically
captured dimension
of divine comprehension
--the non-verbal reality.

One wonders if
the devised construction
even resembles
life's native habitat.
What truth lies
behind the bars?
And can the divine
be reproduced
in caged definition?

chapter 1

Getting Acquainted with God

My family, except for Dad, never missed Quaker meeting unless we were sick. Time in silent worship --open to direction from God took priority over anything else imaginable on Sundays and Wednesdays. Before I could walk, I was carried to the little white meeting house about a quarter of a mile from home. Dad was still living with us then, and although I can't remember it, Mother said he went to meeting with us on Sundays when he could get away from work.

The corporate worship and silence became a comfortable part of me. Occasionally, when the Holy Spirit gave inspiration, some gentle or fiery Quaker would stand and speak or kneel and pray. I didn't understand a whole lot about what was going on inside that very simple sanctuary, but as an adult, I clearly remember the reverent atmosphere, relatively dark interior, and plain benches with long, lumpy cushions from end to end on both sides of a center aisle. Two rows of facing benches allowed elders to sit up front and face the younger worshipers. A black pot-bellied stove stood strategically in the center of the room, offering hand-stoked warmth in winter. Open doors and windows allowed breezes to blow gently through the quiet in summer.

Jesus said, "Let the little children come to me, and do not hinder them for the kingdom of heaven belongs to such as these."

--Matthew 19:14 NIV

I feel austere, yet blessed, just writing about that scene. Once in a while, I would go to sleep leaning against Mother's arm. Sometimes she allowed me to lay my head in her lap. There was something very centered and comfortable in that space. The window straight ahead of the bench where we almost always sat framed a tall tulip tree outside that whispered of changing seasons. In springtime it blossomed in fragrant petal cups of yellow with bands of orange. Then came seed pods that looked like long green pencils. Summer rains rinsed the broad-hand leaves, washed away noise from the road behind us, and drummed refreshing rhythms on the roof and windows. In autumn the tree turned gold; leaves began to fall, lifting the shade, allowing sunlight to focus inside. Winter branches, bare and black, pointed to the sky above and beyond. Snow fell softly on my growing thoughts of God.

Be still and know that I am God...

--Psalm 46:10a NIV

Our family lived on three acres of land between Adena and Harrisville in southeastern Ohio. Out beyond one of our huge gardens was a hillside that nurtured long, soft, orchard grass and a few scrub trees. Mother often took her bible and went out on that hillside to be alone with God, and I decided to try it myself. After the house was cleaned or the dishes done, after the chickens were fed, watered, and the eggs gathered, after the garden was hoed or the vegetables had been picked and preserved, that back pasture field was a comfortable place to lie down, watch the fluffy white clouds, and think God thoughts. Two big poplar trees in the front yard also offered shade and issued invitations for summertime rests on the lawn plus important stimulation for my wondering mind. I felt at home in God's world. God seemed close and good.

Our family bowed heads together in a few moments of *silence* before every meal. This gave us three specific opportunities each day to bow our heads and acknowledge God's provision of food and all the other blessings in our lives. This silent time was an invitation for each family member, in his or her own way, to give thanks and ask God to bless the nourishment we were about to receive. A few Quaker families "set silence" at the end of each meal as well as at the beginning, but ours didn't.

I learned about spoken table prayer the first time I stayed overnight with one of my Mt. Pleasant Elementary School classmates. Her family belonged to the Presbyterian Church in Mt. Pleasant and her father called on her to pray before we ate. Her prayer actually gave words to the gratitude I felt in my heart during our pre-mealtime *silence* at home. I made it a point to memorize the words:

> God is great, God is good and we thank him for
> our food. By his hand we all are fed; give us, Lord,
> our daily bread.

Sometime later I realized how unthinkingly I breezed through memorized prayers when one day I bowed my head at lunchtime and caught myself silently praying other familiar words I'd learned: "Now I lay me down to sleep. . ." I wondered if God noticed. Though no one else at the table had heard, I remember feeling a bit embarrassed.

Mother wanted to teach us to put our trust in God. Each night, I knelt beside the brass-framed double bed that my sister and I shared. Cold linoleum beneath my knees kept my prayer short. "God bless Mamma and Daddy. God bless Marie and Don (my older siblings). And God bless me." She was also the one who taught me to use the prayer that is familiar and often critiqued by many:

> Now I lay me down to sleep; I pray the Lord my soul to keep. If I should die before I wake; I pray thee, Lord, my soul to take.

Obviously those words became a routine prayer habit as evidenced by their already admitted intrusion into the silence of one of my mealtime prayers.

I remember childish delight in finding a variation of that bedtime prayer penciled onto a wooden door of the old Quaker Meeting House near my friend's home in Mt. Pleasant when she and I were poking around that huge, abandoned building. (It had not yet been renovated into the historical landmark that it is today.) Amused, but also a bit offended at the irreverent words that defaced both the prayer and the meeting house, I read:

> Now I lay me down to sleep, a bag of peanuts at my feet. If I should die before I wake, you'll know I died of a belly ache.

I wondered if God thought that was funny. Somehow, I suspected that it made God sad. Mother was pretty circumspect in her view of right and wrong, and we were taught that God wanted us to keep our minds free from idle thoughts and to refrain from naughty deeds –like writing on walls or buildings.

In order to enhance our spiritual development, Mother read to us nearly every night before we went to bed and every Sunday afternoon. She chose stories that taught lessons in faith from a book written especially for children about Old Testament heroes and New Testament followers of Jesus. She also liked stories from a little paper that came regularly through the mail called *John Three Sixteen.*

There's one story I've never been able to forget because of the fear it engendered in my young mind. It was about a woman who, one night when she knelt to pray before getting into bed, felt an unusual urge to pray aloud and ask for God's protection. The notion seemed strange to her; however, she obeyed the inner prompting. After she had finished her prayer and settled herself under the covers, she heard a strange sound. A man who had been hiding under her bed scooted out. He had a knife in his hand and he explained that his original intent had been robbery, but he would have killed her if need be. He confessed that because of her prayer, he simply couldn't follow through with his plan.

I'm certain that what Mother wanted us to learn from that story was that we can be led by the Holy Spirit, that prayer changes things, and that we should have faith in God to protect us from evil. Something like that anyway.

If indeed I learned those things from that story, they were certainly secondary. What I DID learn was that I needed to check under the bed every night to make sure no one was hiding there. Many times I also carefully checked the closet. Even worse than that was the fact that no matter how hot the night in our un-air-conditioned house, I didn't dare let my leg or my arm project out from under the sheet or over the edge of the bed for fear that someone would grab it. At that point in my life, the possibility of a robber hiding under the bed was too much for me to handle –even with prayer.

After we learned to read, Mother enhanced both our attention and our reading ability by letting me and my two siblings take turns reading the daily devotionals aloud from *The Upper Room*, a small Methodist publication that offered (and still offers) a Scripture passage, short reflection or story, a written prayer, and thought for the day.

One of the lessons I learned early on in my Quaker community was respect for all races of people. In fact, Mt. Pleasant was one of the stops on the Underground Railway for slaves seeking freedom. The well-known fact that one of the houses I passed every day on the way to school had secret hiding places in it held great fascination for me. I realize now that these Quakers who took risks in helping slaves escape were actually channels of God's providence for those who sought a better life for themselves and their families.

Every day, our big yellow school bus stopped to pick up boys and girls who lived in a little town called Emerson, a community of former slaves, their children and grandchildren. One of those girls of African heritage became my friendly rival along with another classmate who was an Italian Catholic Democrat. The three of us were an unlikely trio of friends –each doing our best to earn good grades. They usually did better than I, but they expanded my world. (The descendant of slavery later earned a PhD and became Dean of the Nursing School in Cleveland. My Italian friend became a doctor.)

It was when one of my other third-grade classmates died of a burst appendix that I first set foot in an African American Baptist Church. The church was located in Emerson. Students who wanted to attend the funeral (and had obtained written permission from their parents) were transported to and from the little white clapboard church in a school bus. I was so busy absorbing the new experience that I don't remember how many classmates attended, but the church was bulging. It seemed that all the residents of Emerson were there to mourn with the family.

I remember feeling very white. The singing, the mourning,

and the preaching were all very loud. It was quite a contrast from Quaker funerals I'd attended with Mother.

My deceased classmate was wearing a white princess-like dress, quite unlike anything I'd ever seen her wear before, and she was lying in a beautiful coffin. The most haunting memory of that day was the grieving mother's loud plea, which she repeated many times during the service, "Geraldine! Speak to Mommy. Ple-e-ease." I wondered if Geraldine had already seen God in heaven, and if not, just when she'd be getting there. I knew Jesus talked about going to "prepare a place" for his followers, but I didn't know just how those things worked.

Revival meetings at the Harrisville Methodist Church were another source of challenge in my young life. Our grocer was a member of that local Methodist Church and whenever they were having revival services, he made certain that all his customers had an invitation to attend. Mother was open to such things, but the message we children heard at those revival meetings was less familiar.

I remember sitting through the altar calls feeling certain that I should go forward and repent of my sins. But I had no idea what I should confess. If indeed God was displeased with me, I wanted to make things right. But what would I say was wrong? Not finding the insight or the courage to cooperate with what they seemed to think everyone should do, I sat uncomfortably in the pew, wondering if I'd be struck dead as I left and be consigned to eternity in hell. Needless to say, it wasn't a comforting thought.

A lot of the songs sung at those revivals were familiar because my maternal grandmother had been a Methodist before marrying my grandfather. Because of Grandpa's Quaker affiliation and the ultra-conservative rural community in which they lived near Barnesville, OH, they hid their pump organ in the back room. But Mother loved singing the old-time hymns and with limited space at our house, we couldn't hide our organ. It was located in the front bedroom, clearly visible from the living room because the double sliding doors were almost always open. Mother often gathered us around the organ, and later the piano that replaced it, to sing hymns together. She and my sister sang soprano, I sang alto or at least harmonized, and Mother was always prodding my brother, who couldn't read music any better than I, to sing bass.

Though we had no musical instruments in our meeting house and we didn't sing in our worship services, the hymns we sang at home helped to shape our theology. "What a Friend We Have in Jesus" was probably the one we sang most often. Its text underscores the privilege of prayer and the divine assistance that is available.

I vividly remember my first experience of answered prayer --the day prayer really got my heart's attention. I was probably five or six years old. A very special birthday gift of doll booties had come up missing. Beyond anything else, they had made my doll seem more like the real baby I pretended her to be. I searched for days, looking everywhere imaginable. My family helped, but those booties were nowhere to be found.

One night I thought of the booties at prayer time; so, I asked God to help me find them. I have no idea how I thought God might do that or even if I really thought he would. I crawled into bed and promptly went to sleep. Light was streaming through the window when I awoke in the morning and the very first thought that hit my mind was, "Look in the bottom of her bunting." I bounded out of bed and over to my doll's bed. Slipping off her pink flannel bunting, I found just what I had prayed to find. It didn't feel at all like happenstance. I felt certain that God had heard and answered my prayer.

One of our neighbor families attended the Presbyterian Church in Harrisville. Their summertime Daily Vacation Bible School full of lively youngsters was often in need of extra assistance. I was in junior high school when their pastor called and asked if I'd like to be a teacher's assistant in their DVBS program. Every week night for two weeks I rode my red, second-hand bicycle to that church and helped wherever I could. I liked the role and the people. And I liked feeling like a leader.

Questions for Individual Reflection and/or Group Sharing

1. Was there a focus on faith in your childhood? When did you first begin to think about God? Can you describe the circumstance(s)?

2. What was your experience with prayer as a child –in church, at meal-time, bedtime, or any time?

3. How was your early belief about God shaped and nurtured in helpful or unhelpful ways?

4. How did death touch your life and your imagination as a child?

5. What were your experiences with other denominations or religions? How did those influence or affect you?

chapter 2

Heartbreak and God's Providence

Older family members and friends of my parents have told me in times past that Dad and Mom had seemed like an ideal couple. They met at Olney, a private boarding school sponsored by the Ohio Yearly Meeting of Friends at Barnesville, OH. Before Mother died at age ninety-four, I spent hours at the nursing home reading aloud Dad's love letters to her –letters written in the late 1920's. She had carefully boxed and tied them with ribbons to keep forever just as she cherished and honored the vows she made to him on their wedding day in 1929.

We children never heard harsh words between them, but we couldn't help noticing Mother's frequent tears. It was at least a couple of years before Mother told us what was making her sad, but we were not uninformed. Children have ways of discovering and discussing hidden truths among themselves. On our own, we managed to break the code in Mother's personal diary.

As Dad's "secret" affair progressed, Mom found lipstick on one of his handkerchiefs. Mother didn't wear lipstick. Then there was a bottle of liquor in the car. We Quakers didn't use alcoholic beverages. Another time, we found a pair of some lady's panties in the glove box of the car. Remembering all this with Mother later, she told me that Dad was clearly trying to give her cause to divorce him because he had no court-supported "cause" to divorce her. In fact, there were many times when he told her and members of his family that she was the best, most loyal and hardworking wife any man could ever want.

So what was the problem? Had I the insight then that I've gleaned over the years of family heartbreak and from the love letters that Mother shared with me, I've come to the conclusion that though they lived quite happily under the rules and regulations of the boarding school while they were students together, that sort of conservatism was too much for Dad. His family was simply more liberal than Mother's family. There were many things that Dad wanted to do, like going to movies and dances, that Mother (as well as most Fundamentalists of that day) felt were wrong. She could not conscientiously participate. So, a man who worked for Dad found Dad a playmate who was glad to do the things Mother couldn't. I've been told that Dad warned the woman, who had been married twice before, that this was not to be a serious affair because he had a wonderful wife and family at home, but she wasn't about to let Dad go once she had him in her clutches.

There was another issue that undoubtedly caused division. The Second World War was raging. Mother's brother, a conscientious objector to war, was serving time in prison because he refused to register for the draft. Although Quakers were strong proponents of Pacifism and non-cooperation with the war effort, Dad was obviously embarrassed that his brother-in-law was a CO and in prison.

Dad's family undoubtedly wanted peace as much as Mom's family, but they chose to work at it in different ways. Dad's younger brother was serving in Germany with General Patton and one of his younger sister's husband was serving in the Philippines.

(I know what Dad thought about conscientious objectors to war because in 1954 during the Korean War, my fiancé could legally

*register as a CO. Stan and I were planning to be married and I wanted him to meet my dad. When Dad learned that we were going into Alternative Service, he rudely told us in blustering and no uncertain terms, "I wish **I'd** been drafted! I'd have shown them that I didn't have a yellow streak down **my** back.")*

Our family of five, including my older siblings, Marie and Don, used to make Sunday trips to visit Mom's parents in Barnesville about thirty miles away, but then Dad began "needing to work" on Sundays and the four of us went alone. One Sunday when we returned home, we found that Dad had taken all his things and moved out.

We prayed many prayers for Dad to come back to us. And I naively thought that he surely would. Alas, that never happened. Reflecting now, I sense the tension between our will, what we believed to be God's will, and Dad's free will. Prayer is not about getting our own way but about opening our hearts to find God's way, which is Love's way, for our lives.

In 1946 Dad filed for divorce himself. The reason stated on the official documents and in the newspaper was "gross neglect of duty." To the court and to Mother that was interpreted as denial of conjugal rights. For the court, that was reason enough. For Mother, it represented a bald-faced lie. For Dad, I now think it must have meant that Mother was not the life-companion that they had promised to be for each other in the marriage vows. He obviously wanted a wife who would/could share in the things he wanted to do for fun and recreation.

This was in the 1940's and divorce was unheard of in our community, although we knew that such things happened in Hollywood. Divorce still carried a huge stigma of shame and failure. Mother endured personal despair while living under community scrutiny and wonderment. She sealed us in a protective silence, not wanting to do or say anything that would harm Dad's respectability or make it harder for him to change his ways and come back to us. We were living in fertile ground where low self-worth could flourish. But there is one thing about this whole experience for which I will be eternally grateful: In spite of all our Dad did that was wrong, Mother taught us to love and forgive him. What he did was not right, but we were not to hate him.

Quakers taught that disputes should be settled out of court and Mother did not contest the divorce or ask for anything in settlement. Dad's attorney wrote Mom a letter that I discovered after her death. In it he told her that this was the strangest divorce case he'd ever handled because at no time did Dad say anything bad about her. He added, "Mr. Bundy said that you are a truly good woman." The court awarded Mom our three-acre home place with two huge gardens, a small orchard, barn, two chicken houses, an old shop building, our four-room house with no bathroom, our decrepit Oldsmobile, and $20 a month for each child until we reached the age of eighteen.

Mother felt that with three children to raise and nurture, she should not seek outside employment. She was a hard worker and she was a woman of faith. It was a familiar sight to find her in the living room with her bible when we got up in the mornings. I know she was seeking direction on her lonely tear-filled journey.

> ***So do not worry, saying, 'What shall we eat?' or 'What shall we drink?' or 'What shall we wear?' For the pagans run after all these things, and your heavenly Father knows that you need them. But seek first his kingdom and his righteousness, and all these things will be given to you as well.***
>
> **--Matthew 6: 31-33 NIV**

It was nothing for us to still be working at midnight in the summertime. Mother wanted our garden and orchard produce to be canned or frozen at prime picking times. We did not lack for good nutrition. Of course we ate lots of eggs and there was chicken every Sunday.

Our laundry equipment consisted of long clotheslines in the back yard, an old Maytag wringer washer and two big rinse tubs side-by-side on a large wooden box that sat on our closed-in back porch. So, we took in laundry too. Mother was as meticulous about the ironing as about everything else, and my sister and I were part of Mother's laundry team.

Our family served as custodians for the meeting house and cemetery. My brother mowed other people's yards with our push mower. He also helped a neighboring farmer every summer when it was time to bale hay, and he often came home with a bad headache from working all day in the dust and sun. Mother counted on him to be "the man of the house" but often helped him to do some of the dirtiest work: shoveling coal into the cellar bin for our hot air furnace as well as cleaning out the chicken houses and our outdoor toilet.

My sister and I baby sat whenever we had a chance. Mother taught us to sew and we made nearly all our clothes --some of them out of printed cloth sacks that the chicken feed came in. Our local 4-H Club also challenged us to perfect our skills and provided good times as well.

We worked with Mother and she also liked to play with us. When we needed a work break or on Sunday afternoons, we'd have a game of soft ball or gypsy tag in the front yard. Neighbor children often came to play as well. While snapping beans, shelling peas, or cutting apples we'd play word games that were fun and undoubtedly improved our spelling. While dressing chickens or doing dishes, Mother would have us singing and harmonizing together. I think she often sang her blues away.

We didn't have much money to spend, but we had a Mother who loved us and a God who helped us. If there were government welfare programs in those days, we knew nothing about them. Mother must have known, though, that God helps those who try to help themselves. I'm sure our praying Mother kept God informed about needs that were more than she could handle.

Our sixteen-year-old Oldsmobile not only guzzled gas, it was forever breaking down or having a flat tire. Years before Daddy left us, I overheard him talking with someone about the fact that the car's rear-end was loose and might come off if it wasn't repaired. We three children always sat in the back seat when the whole family was going somewhere and I remember being afraid that the car would break apart and leave us sitting in the road while he and Mom drove on ahead.

Either the car wasn't repaired at that time or it needed fixing again because I well recall the time (after Dad was gone) when Mother took it to the repair shop for some other reason and just as it was centered over the hydraulic lift, the rear-end mechanism fell off. I can still hear it hitting the floor. How much more timely could that complete breakdown have been? It meant more expense, but at least we weren't at home or out on the open road.

There were always things that needed to be fixed at home as well. Mother tried to keep up with the bills, but sometimes creditors had to wait for a month or so. One time we had an unusually large car repair bill to pay --$118 to be exact. And we had no money to pay it. Mother had been trying to figure out how to cut corners or earn some extra cash. I'll never forget it because one day, before we'd been able to get it paid, Mother went out to get the mail and in it she found a letter addressed to her and a check from a concerned Quaker in another state. We didn't know the man so I don't remember his name, but I remember what he wrote. "Dear Friend: I am feeling that thee might be in some sort of financial need. Please accept the enclosed check to help out wherever necessary." The check was for exactly $118. We all felt that we'd experienced a miracle.

Mother wanted all three of us to get our high school education at Olney, the Quaker boarding school she and Dad, as well as all our other uncles and aunts, had attended. She wanted us to be in an environment where Christian values would be taught and where we wouldn't be tempted by Hollywood movies, public school proms, alcohol, or cigarettes. To this day, I don't know how she managed to pay for Marie's and Don's four years of private schooling except that they each had paying jobs on campus during the school year and then used the money they'd earned in the summers to help Mom pay their tuition, room, and board. I don't know whether they received additional financial aid or not. In those days, I'd never heard of available financial aid.

The summer after I had finished eighth grade, Walter Brown, a traveling Quaker minister who also owned a basket factory in North Carolina, visited our meeting and took note of our family –especially me. He was a strong supporter of the school and somehow he realized what a financial burden Mother was carrying. I think he also resonated with her sense of responsibility for our Christian upbringing.

One week before the school year was to begin, I spoke to the school matron about needing and not having a work assignment for the coming year. She was surprised that I didn't already know that Walter Brown had made prior arrangements for me. "He wants thee to be free to focus on learning and other aspects of life here at Olney, and he will be paying thy tuition, room, and board for all four years." What a surprise! What a blessing! It seemed too good to be true. Talk about God's provision! This was as much a help to Mother as it was to me.

> ***Trust in the Lord, and do good; so you will dwell in the land, and enjoy security. Take delight in the Lord and he will give you the desires of your heart. Commit your way to the Lord; trust in him, and he will act.***
>
> **--Psalm 37:3-5 RSV**

I loved life at boarding school. I wasn't at the top scholastically, but I thrived on extra-curricular activities, participating in speaking contests, leading the singing at campfires and group "sings," playing girls' basketball and field hockey, taking turns at chairing the Literary Society, and always being involved in the Student Government Association which was often called Self-Gov.

My sister had been a leader in Self-Gov when she was there and my brother, still a student my first two years there, was a leader as well. I started out as the freshman representative on the Coordinating Committee that received and dealt with reports of rule infractions such as making too much noise in the dorm or being out of one's room after "lights out," skipping meeting, morning or evening collection, or study halls –all of which were monitored by students. (Students, faculty and staff all gathered in what was called the "collecting room" for morning and evening bible reading, five or ten minutes of silent reflection, and then any announcements that needed to be made.) Roommates were responsible for cleaning their own rooms. Once every week, two boys graded the girls' rooms while two girls checked out the boys' housekeeping habits. Public, and often humorous, reports were made then at the weekly association meeting. Student Government officers were responsible for divvying up all other rotating cleaning assignments on campus, including a "dish crew" that cleaned up after meals and reset the tables. All but the most serious breaches of school regulations were handled by Student Government. Probably the highest honor a senior could receive was to be elected by the whole student body to be the Boys' or Girls' Director of this student association. I remember feeling complete shock when I was chosen, but I took my role seriously and enjoyed it.

As my boarding school days came to a close, I realized how rich and full my four years had been--and how empty and undirected I felt as I faced the future looming ahead, knowing that I couldn't afford a college education. My steady boyfriend of three years had graduated the year before and was studying at Earlham College. Many, including me, felt sure we'd be married someday, but he had three more years of college, and he wanted his future wife to have a college education.

In a sociology class late in my senior year, Teacher Worth Mackey gave us statistics which indicated that children of divorced parents are likely to have unhappy marriages themselves, resulting in yet another generation of broken homes. That prediction caught me emotionally off-guard. Again I felt like I was damaged merchandise. I didn't dare breathe for fear I would choke on restrained sobs. Mercifully, the bell rang for class to end. I hurried to the door, tears spilling down my cheeks.

The principal's office was just across the hall and Teacher Byron Thomas, the principal, happened to be standing in his doorway, casually watching classes dismiss. He was a man I highly respected –maybe even loved because of his obvious faith and sensitive caring for others. He reached out and gently pulled me aside. Taking me into his office and closing the door, he asked what was wrong. I told him about the statistics we'd just been given. "If I really love Jay," I confessed, "I won't marry him and risk messing up his life." Teacher Byron's warm brown eyes looked straight into mine. "Ruth," he said, "the very fact that you care this much means that you will work extra hard to see that your own marriage lasts." I don't remember anything else that might have been said by either of us, but I can still see his lean, lanky body language speaking of compassion and full acceptance. I have never forgotten that day or his comforting words. Surely God used Teacher Byron to give me hope that could help heal my wounded heart.

Graduation day was coming far too fast. I knew the time had come for me to take charge of my future, but I didn't know where to start. Like many of the other seniors, I had pored over Lovejoy's Book of Colleges and I'd written to several for information and applications, but it all seemed so hopeless. My sister and brother had wanted to go to college too, but there was no family support for them or for me to accomplish that dream.

At least twice, I slipped away by myself and sat on the hillside overlooking the hockey field. Tears came easily. "Oh God, I feel so terribly alone as I face the future."

Questions for Individual Reflection and/or Group Sharing:

1. What obstacles/challenges did you or your family of origin face?

2. Did prayer or faith play a part in helping the family to cope or to find solutions?

3. As you reflect on your youth, who were outstanding channels of God's providence for you? In what way(s)? Did you realize it at the time or only as you reflect on your past?

4. What values learned while growing up in your family of origin have significantly shaped who you have become or are becoming?

chapter 3

God Speaks Clearly –But Not Always

Although everyone in my immediate family had graduated from high school, none had gone on to a four-year or liberal arts college. The prospect of getting family support for my growing desire to get more education was very dim.

My sister, Marie, had taken a short secretarial course at a community college as soon as she graduated and was now employed. I remember that one of her first paychecks went to help purchase new inlaid linoleum for the kitchen. Mother had painted the old worn out covering a number of times to keep it looking as nice as she could but it didn't stay nice very long.

When my brother graduated, he immediately got a position as a bank teller and started saving his salary to replace the family car. Living back at home, both of them helped Mother with ever-present repair and upkeep expenses on our little four room house with a path instead of a bath.

Since both of my siblings were older and I was away at school, Mother started a new vocation doing practical nursing for elderly folks in the community and often beyond. Depending upon the level of patient care needed, she was sometimes gone 24/7. By this time, any of the three of us could handle things at home when needed, but this didn't mean that more money was available.

Mother had just changed the way she earned a living –no longer feeling that she needed to be at home.

But financial backing wasn't my only problem. Like many conservatives of that day, Mother was concerned that her children might lose their faith if they went to college and were exposed to academic freedom of thought. She didn't overtly try to stop me from pursuing the possibility of going to college, but she would still be ready to veto plans that she felt were certain to be detrimental. The benefactor who paid my way for boarding school had not offered to send me on to college.

My paternal grandfather was my buddy while I was growing up. Grandpa and Grandma Bundy lived less than a mile away because Mom had moved to Dad's community when they were married. Grandpa tried to fill in some of the empty spots in my life which Dad's leaving had created. Grandpa took me and my friends roller skating a number of times and just sat on the sidelines watching us have fun. It was Grandpa who, without Mother's knowledge, took me to my first movie. It was Grandpa who taught me to drive in his new Packard, never reprimanding --just squeezing his knee nervously when he thought I was going too fast. I could easily read his body language.

Grandpa took Mother's side in our family break-up, but he and Dad were still in business together and he worked with Dad every weekday. I couldn't ask Grandpa for money. It wouldn't have been fair because I was just one of his almost twenty grandchildren; but a logical solution to my financial problem dawned on me: *Why not ask Grandpa to ask Dad if he'd be willing to help me go to college?* I had no way of knowing, but I figured that Grandpa had told Dad about the good high school experience all three of his children had had at boarding school –Dad's own alma mater. I reasoned to myself: *How could a dad help but be pleased and at least a little proud? He just might decide to help fund further growth whether his current wife wanted him to or not.*

Grandpa agreed to ask, but the report he brought back to me was short. Dad had said, "You tell Ruth that women are supposed to get married and raise a family. Women don't need college." Thus, I knew there would be no assistance from Dad. I wasn't into begging.

Discouraged, but not completely daunted, I studied materials I'd received from the fifteen colleges and universities I'd contacted earlier as a result of studying Lovejoy's book on colleges. I checked prices, available scholarships and work opportunities. I ended up dismissing all the State schools because if Mother was ever to be happy with my choice of college, it would need to have a church affiliation.

I couldn't really consider Earlham because my steady boyfriend was already a student there. Mother was very fond of him, but she worried that without strict social rules, such as we had at boarding school, we'd not be able to handle the temptations that come with greater freedom. Besides, it was one of the more expensive private colleges. If they had jobs available on campus, I didn't know about it and I figured that their scholastic standards were too high for me to get a scholarship.

I not only needed tuition, room and board, I needed money for clothes, books, and supplies as well. On paper, Wilmington looked like a possibility because of its highly advertised work-study program. One of my sister's best friends had married the admissions director there and he encouraged us to visit the campus. I felt sure he'd have a personal interest in answering our questions and helping me find financial aid and employment. It was mid-June already when we got out the map and found our way to Wilmington. Mother was still holding the school in abeyance because she'd heard they allowed dancing on campus. I tried to be considerate of her feelings even though I had a sense of rhythm that would have lent itself well to dancing. I figured she'd had enough to worry about over the years and I didn't want to give her new cause to worry. I'm sure that both of us were silently praying that we would be given the wisdom and direction we needed that day as well as whatever future assistance was necessary.

I was not ready for the feeling that came over me as we drove through the campus entrance. I hardly know how to describe it. I was expecting a rush of excitement. Instead, a sort of gray pall fell over me. We were given the royal treatment that admissions officers give to students, but there was absolutely no joy in my heart; it was hard for me to even listen to the things that were being said. I knew that was not the place for me.

> ***Trust in the Lord with all your heart and lean not on your own understanding; in all your ways submit to him, and he will make your paths straight.***
>
> **--Proverbs 3:5-6 NIV**

Back at home, I was one discouraged teenager. "God, I've done everything I know and I'm getting nowhere. If you want me to go to college, you're going to have to show me how and where."

It seemed that my prayers for guidance were not being answered. Sitting in our meeting for worship the next Wednesday morning, the familiar silence settled around me and the other worshipers. My mind released my worry and was actually empty of other thought. I think I entered a twilight zone similar to that which is between being awake and being asleep. By that time I wasn't even expecting to receive guidance. Somewhere near the end of the hour, something like a light went on in my head and while I am certain that there were no audible words, I heard them spoken clearly in my mind.

"LOOK AT THE LITTLE BROWN BULLETIN." I was instantly alert. I knew exactly which little brown bulletin was intended. It was the one I had ignored because it was small, a bit drab looking, and it was from a Class B school. Everything was less expensive, but the college was not fully accredited. Nevertheless, because of the way the suggestion had come, I could hardly wait to get home. I knew all the college catalogues I'd ordered earlier were together in a box under my bed.

The minute I got in the house, I made a bee-line for the bedroom. I randomly opened that "little brown bulletin" and the first thing I saw was: "Code of Conduct." Clearly outlined were the answers to many things that Mother cared about: No dancing, smoking or drinking on campus. I knew little about the denominational background of the school except that I knew Mennonites were what we Quakers called one of the three traditional "Peace" churches. That was something that I valued. Quite frankly, I also appreciated the "no smoking or drinking" rule. Those practices were no-no's in my code of conduct as well. I could live without dancing. Much more important: Would I be able to get a scholarship and a job?

I promptly completed the application for admission form that was in the book and sent it with a transcript and letter of inquiry about financial aid. Then I went to live with Uncle Wilson Morlan and his family near Salem, OH, for the rest of the summer. Aunt Edna, one of Dad's sisters, was having surgery and needed someone to take over the household for a couple of months. I was happy to have paid employment for the summer and they were a generous loving couple who, with their three young children, modeled a truly wonderful family life.

Within a couple of weeks Dr. Paul R. Shelly, Head of the

Bluffton College Bible Department, came knocking at the door. It was July. --A little late to be making arrangements for college that fall and very late to be asking for special financial considerations. We had no idea that anyone was coming. I was dressed in homemade shorts, cleaning underneath the kitchen sink when he arrived. He explained that he was helping out in the Admissions Department for the summer. I invited him into the living room and we sat down. He had a sort of squinty twitch that jumped between his eye and the corner of his mouth. I wondered if he was as nervous as I was.

One of the first things he asked me was why I had applied to Bluffton College? There was my first challenge. Was I going to tell him about my unusual experience in meeting or was I going to give him some response that I thought might be more typical and less mystical? I decided to be honest and play it straight.

Dr. Shelly kept smiling, twitching, and nodding his head as though he understood what I was saying. He didn't ask anything about the transcript or my extracurricular activities; those things he already had in hand. And it wasn't long at all before he stood to leave. "Ruth," he said, "I know you are eligible for a scholarship. You can count on that. But campus jobs were assigned a couple of weeks ago and I'm not at all sure whether I can arrange anything there or not. Let me go back and see if there are any possibilities. I'll be in touch either way."

The week flew by. His letter came while I was dusting books in Uncle Wilson's personal library. The news in a nutshell was that I was to be his secretary every afternoon after classes. He'd also arranged for me to work in the Registrar's office every Saturday morning --typing and mimeographing the Sunday worship bulletin for First Mennonite Church in town.

When my brother heard the news, he said, "Well, if you are going to college, I am too." He quit his job at the bank, and in

September the two of us loaded all our things into his car and headed across the state for Bluffton College --a place neither of us had seen before the day we unpacked on campus. He got a job with the Omar Bakery delivering bread in the very early morning hours before classes.

I didn't give any more thought to the fact that the school we had chosen was not fully accredited until a chapel program early in the fall of our sophomore year. President Lloyd L. Ramseyer, smiling broadly, approached the podium to share his joy: "We have received a report from the North Central Association study and I am pleased to announce that Bluffton College has now been approved for full accreditation." Obviously the All-knowing One knew I didn't need to worry about Bluffton's being a Class B school at the time I applied. Unbeknownst to me, plans were already underway for that to change. Another thing I didn't know at the time was how my two jobs at the college would be connected to my future. But that will come later in my story.

As for my relationship with Jay, out-of-sight for too long a time can also lead to out-of-mind. We'd not only been apart while he was at Earlham my senior year at Olney, he had taken a summer job as a camp counsellor at Camp Dark Waters in New Jersey for that summer. I got tired of being apart all the time even though we wrote letters and still had a special relationship. I dated other fellows just for fun. Nothing serious. Eventually, however, I accepted the class ring of another fellow I liked a lot at Bluffton.

That ring is the subject of another encounter with what seemed to be a God thing.

By the spring of our freshman year at college, one of my friends and I were both part of the advisory cabinet for the Student Christian Association on campus. We were participating in an all-day Sunday retreat. The whole cabinet had been transported in a couple of college cars to a farm a few miles away.

It was a lovely day and as we sat in the sunshine for morning worship together, I removed my watch and Stan's ring so the tan on my arms and fingers would be even. (Stan was my steady boyfriend at Bluffton.) I slipped both pieces of jewelry into the pocket of my shirt. After our picnic lunch and before our afternoon planning session, we horsed around doing cartwheels, backbends, and somersaults in the huge front yard that stretched between the house and barn.

Later, as our afternoon meetings were winding down, I reached in my pocket to retrieve my watch and ring but the ring was gone. I panicked inside. It had to have dropped out while we were playing on the lawn. The grass was long waiting for a first mowing of the season. Where would I even begin to look for the ring? How could I tell Stan that I had lost the ring he treasured, yet gave me to wear? I tuned in to hear the SCA president saying, "We're going to close with another brief time of worship. Let's begin with a few minutes of silence, then we'll sing, and I'll close with prayer. When we're finished, you must promptly gather up your things and go directly to the cars because we need to get back to campus in time for supper." There I was, sitting cross-legged on the flat concrete surrounding a small fish pond in the farmer's backyard, the afternoon sun reflecting off the solid white surface.

That worship time was filled with mental chaos for me. "Oh God, what am I going to do? I couldn't find my way back to this farm even if I had a car. And besides, by the time I could get back here, it will be too dark to look for anything. Oh God! O my God, how could I have been so careless as to lose Stan's ring?" I don't think I even prayed that God would help me find the ring –that seemed an impossibility. And certainly, I didn't hear any direction from God. My mind wasn't quiet enough to even listen for or to hear the still small voice.

The first thing I did after the chairperson's "amen" was to

frantically tell my best friend about my loss. She was concerned, but had her own things to gather up. I walked quickly but hopelessly out to the center of the yard on my way to the cars. As my friend was just coming around the corner of the house, she called to me by my nickname, "Bunnie, did you find Stan's ring?" I stopped and turned to answer her ridiculous question. Of course I hadn't found it. I hadn't even had time to look for it. "No," I said, tears stinging my eyes. Just as I said it, I looked to the ground where I was standing and there. . . Yes, THERE was the ring gleaming brightly up at me. I grabbed it and ran to get in the car.

Back at the dorm, my friend and I held each other and sobbed with joy over what seemed to both of us to be much more mysterious than happenstance. If she hadn't called and stopped me at that very moment, I would have missed it.

God, however, does not always intervene or provide the help we want when we want it. Such seemed to be the case a year or so later when I seriously wanted God's help in deciding whom I should marry. Sometime in the autumn of my sophomore year and Stan's senior year, he asked for his class ring back –in order, I think, to make sure there wasn't something better among the new class of freshman girls. He wanted to date around, including me but not exclusively with me. I soon learned that I needed to quit having occasional dates with Stan if I wanted others to ask me out. I quit saying yes to Stan's invitations. It worked quite well.

By Christmastime another student who lived off-campus (a returned veteran) had asked me to marry him. He was a nice guy and I'd had great fun with him, but deep inside I knew that we weren't "made for each other." First of all and important to me, he was not a pacifist. He also claimed that he had quit smoking in order to please me, but one night I found a pack of cigarettes in his shirt pocket.

By that time, Stan was back and certain that I was the one

for him. He was the sort of gentleman I really liked. But Jay still weighed into the mix as well. I loved Stan and Jay for different reasons. Stan was a practical, take charge sort of person who took pride in his work as a janitor in College Hall; he kept the floors waxed and highly polished. Jay was a poet at heart, a romantic like me. I loved the letters he wrote. They made me feel loved. Stan's letters, written in the summertime when we were apart, sounded a bit like job reports. Still I liked the fact that he seemed to be at home in the work-a-day world; furthermore, he was ready for marriage.

I laid out my case in prayer: "But, God, both of them make me feel loved when we're together. And we wouldn't be depending on letters to communicate if we were married. Are Jay and I too much alike? How would he handle the mundane matters of life? I had no way of knowing. Maybe I need someone unlike me to complement my own weaknesses. Help me think through this, God. Please?"

Another complicating matter was the fact that Walter Brown, my boarding school benefactor, had sent me a picture of one of his grandsons who lived in North Carolina and was attending Guilford College. He'd told me a year or two before that he wanted us to meet. Along with the photograph he said he believed we might discover that God had a fine future for us together. It was clear that marriage was what he had in mind. His grandson was nice looking, but we'd never had occasion to meet. In a way, I felt a responsibility to at least consider my benefactor's wishes; after all, I respected him and he seemed to have been Spirit-led when he helped me financially. But I didn't want to feel that I'd been bought. "O God, do you have something better planned for me than the two young men I already really like and even love? Am I being unfair to Walter Brown if I make a choice without ever meeting his grandson? Would he just complicate my choice?"

I took Stan home for a week-end visit after Mother had already known Jay for three years. She liked both of them. Laughingly she quipped, using the King James pronoun that Quakers used and many still use, "Ruth, don't be bringing in any more boyfriends. Thee's getting me confused. I don't know who I like best."

Stan wanted me to marry him after his graduation and go into Alternative Service with him. Jay was taking a break from college and was doing his Alternative Service in Puerto Rico.

I was as much a pacifist as either of them and I welcomed a chance to let my life speak. Women my age had opinions about violence and war --even if the government wasn't requiring us to register for the military draft. Another factor in this whole "marriage mix" was the fact that I had to borrow $500 from Grandpa Bundy to finish out my sophomore year at college and that seemed like a huge amount of debt. It was frightening to think about having to borrow still more in the future. I didn't think I could financially manage to go back to school in the fall. Maybe it was time to get married. "O God, give me direction. Tell me what to do. What is your will for me? Just say the word or give me a clear sign" --such as I'd heard about in family living class.

Miss Edna Ramseyer, my home economics professor, had taken our small family living class to visit Dr. Ella Bauman, a highly respected missionary who was on furlough and currently living in town. I remember only one story that Dr. Ella told us; it had to do with God's direction after she was already preparing to be a missionary doctor. The young man she was dating was not preparing for mission work and she did not see how his planned-for career would fit with her sense of call. One day while she was considering this matter, she clearly heard a voice that said, "Harvey Bauman will be your husband." She was amazed –first of all because no one else was in the house, and she knew she had heard that voice. Secondly, although Harvey Bauman was also planning to be a missionary doctor, he was in a serious relationship with someone else. She didn't explain how it all worked out, but when she told us this story, she and Dr. Harvey Bauman had been married for many years, serving together in India. Two of their daughters were students in our class that day.

If such clear word came to guide my choice of a husband, I didn't hear it. Perhaps a major difference between my prayer about college and my prayer about a husband was that with the former, I simply had no way or wisdom of my own, but when it came to husbands, I had options.

> **I distrust those people who know so well what God wants them to do because I notice it always coincides with their own desires.**
>
> **--Susan B Anthony, reformer and suffragist (1820-1906)**

The above quote from Susan B. Anthony has caused me to reflect again about my own sense of God's direction in my life. If I put that beside **Psalm 37:4,** ***"Delight yourself in the Lord and he will give you the desires of your heart,"*** I must ask myself whether my own desires and scriptural heart desires are the same thing. Up to this point in my life, it is true that discovering God's providence or direction through prayer did usually end up opening a path in at least the general direction I thought I wanted to go.

It is possible that God was speaking to me through my boarding school benefactor, but his voice didn't carry the same emotional weight that I'd experienced in God's past leading. After he heard that I was engaged, he wrote to me expressing his disappointment and asking that I wait. I knew he wanted me to wait until I'd had a chance to meet his grandson. Alas, I was already choosing between two fine young men. A third would possibly/probably confuse me more. Much as I respected Walter Brown, I just wasn't ready for a matchmaker to arrange my social life or marriage, and I was feeling a bit manipulated even if my feelings were not justified.

It seemed God's silence in this matter was saying to me that this choice was mine –a choice I was free to make and then live with.

In the end, one suitor was more persistent (and more ready for marriage) than the other. I finally found myself praying, "God, if it is not your will for me to marry Stan, please stop me."

Stan graduated in May of 1954 and in late September, we were married. Even the sleepless night before my wedding, I was praying --hoping that I wasn't making a mistake.

Questions for Individual Reflection or Group Sharing:

1. What issues were you bringing to God when you were a young adult?

2. Did God help direct you through this important stage of life? How?

3. Can you see ways in which God may have directed you or provided for you without your asking for it?

4. Did prayer enter into your decisions or concerns about marriage?

5. What is your response to the apparent dichotomy between Susan B. Anthony's quotation and Psalm 37:4? Does God have a preference about whom we marry?

chapter 4

Serving and Learning to Pray Aloud

In the last months of his senior year at college, Stan had been working through Mennonite Central Committee to plan for his alternative to military service. MCC had made arrangements for him to serve in the business office at Brooklane Farm in Maryland, a facility for the mentally ill.

The Maryland assignment sounded like a good fit for Stan since he was graduating with a degree in business. Room and board would be provided and his salary was to be $17.00 per week. He was pleased that he would be spending the required two years working in his field of interest. The one catch was that Brooklane Farm had no provision for married couples. Stan would be required to live with the other young men employed at the farm who were also classified by the government as 1-W's –working at alternative assignments because of their opposition to war. I'm sure that the prayer of my heart at that time was not that I could go with him; that had already been determined. But I did want his assignment to work out for everyone's best --something we didn't always understand.

When he reported this MCC arrangement to his draft board, they told him he couldn't take the position in Maryland because they needed more service workers in his home state of Indiana. In order to cooperate with the government, he simply replied, "Please tell me then where I am to serve." He was assigned to menial work copying hand-written menus for the dietary department at Methodist Hospital in Indianapolis.

The hospital did not provide room and board, but because of the required change of plans, we would be able to begin our married life together. His first trip to Indianapolis was to complete paperwork with the hospital Personnel Director. When finished, Stan showed him a picture of me and asked, "Would you have a job for her as well?" Unusual as that sort of employment application seemed to be, we both had jobs waiting for us following our September wedding and honeymoon.

We rented a $60 a month efficiency apartment above a garage on Valley Avenue. We drove to work together each day in our second-hand, royal blue Buick and usually ate lunch together in the hospital cafeteria. It wasn't long until Stan was transferred to the hospital payroll department, a 1-W position that he could enjoy.

My first assignment there was in the hospital lab office, but a few months later I was offered a job as stenographer in the superintendent's office --transcribing and typing all of his and the assistant superintendent's letters. The promotion came with a heads-up admission that the position was a hard one for them to keep filled because the long-time administrative assistant in that office was a very demanding and difficult woman.

My greatest joy came when our two-year term of service was over and she planned a lovely office party in my honor. It was then that the assistant superintendent, who was about ten years older than I, confessed that he had never respected conscientious objectors and the 1-W men who worked there. He figured that they were just draft dodgers. But as he had learned to know me personally, he began to see that CO's were serious about wanting to be peacemakers. I felt my time there had been worthwhile.

Following the required two years of alternative service, we moved to Ligonier, Indiana where Stan had found employment as a time management engineer. Our daughter was born there and we marveled at the miracle of creation that she represented. It was with a full heart that I took baby Kim out for sunshiny afternoon strolls down South Main in her red and white checkered stroller. Life could not have been more idyllic and we were truly grateful.

A few months later, an economic recession was in full swing and the Essex Wire plant was laying off scores of their employees. Stan was among them. Shortly after that, the company was completely closed. Jobs were hard to find. Stan checked back with a company in Fort Wayne that had contacted him when he was graduating from college. The pay was not great, but it was better than not having a job. We made the difficult decision to put our thirteen-month old daughter in day care and I went to work too --at the same company. We had only one car. After about two weeks and many tears, both daughter and mother adjusted to the new arrangement.

I enjoyed my work as an administrative assistant and respected the vice-president who was my boss and was very active in his church. Stan and I were now able to begin purchasing our first home. To be honest I need to admit that the warm relationship between my boss and me eventually became uncomfortable. It was nothing sexual –just far too frequently and demonstratively affectionate. Today, this kind of relationship between men in powerful positions and the women who work for them is openly recognized and condemned as being abuse of power and position. Years later, I reflected on the situation in this poem:

Delayed Testimony

You died before Anita Hill
took our Supreme Judge to court.
You are concealed now
behind a drapery
unlike the one you used to pull
to hide your affections
expressed so gently
with love --age for youth.

You dangled lunches
and privilege
before my assistant eyes,
giving me gifts
which my husband
could ill afford.

I left your grasp
which first felt friendly
to me, whose father left me
wanting
to be loved by an older man
--successful and rich.

The wealth of the years
and the wisdom of leaving you
--as I did--
comes back for trial today.
If I had known then
what I know now,
would I have walked away
so quietly?

It was 1960 and if Stan suspected anything inappropriate was going on, he never mentioned it. Neither did I. After all, many of the perks I was receiving were benefiting him as well. We were often invited to hob-nob with the top executives at their card parties. But my conscience told me that things between me and my boss had gotten out of hand. I could no longer live knowing that we needed to hide, from our spouses and others, what was going on at the office.

Fortunately, Stan and I both realized that since we wanted two children and we wanted them to be able to enjoy each other, we needed to do something about it soon. I also knew that pregnancy would be my perfect "out" for leaving my job with no hard feelings. When my boss found out that I was thinking of becoming a full-time wife and mother, he offered a leave of absence and a better salary. When I turned that down, the president of the company asked me to come back as his own administrative assistant. That was tempting, but my boss was clearly offended that I'd even consider such an offer.

This was a transitional time. The temptation of more money was strong. I was secretary of the Fort Wayne Business Personnel Club at the time and knew the human resource director at Lincoln Life. He too offered me a job with more money.

I prayed that God would somehow make clear to me what I should do. That clarity came when I held our newborn son in my arms. I had just a little over a year and a half until Kim would be in kindergarten. If I wanted time with my children, I was going to have to take it. We'd find some way to live within one income.

My boss was interested in writing poetry and he'd published a number of articles in his church's denominational magazine. As a going away gift, he gave me a leather notebook full of empty pages. On the first one he wrote that I should use it to write about my own Christian beliefs and experiences. That was reinforcement for an interest I already possessed.

My first poem was written around 2:00 A.M. one Sunday morning just after I finished reading Thomas Kelly's *Testament of Devotion.* I submitted it to a Catholic magazine. It was published and I received a small check.

Perspective

Hemmed in my duty
Days are heavy paced
And slow.
Our lives are bound
Until we learn
The purpose
Of all need.

God meets us there
In the commonplace.
Often He does not change
The circumstance—
But alters instead
Our cloudy view.

We find
True freedom
In commitment.

The essence of our being
We find
In service.

One of my first articles was titled "Golden October" and it

was about relishing irreplaceable time with my children. A Baptist magazine published it. I was one happy wife and mother!

Church was important to both Stan and me. While still living in Indianapolis, we were active in the programed First Friends Church, and during our year in Ligonier the Methodists made us feel at home. In Fort Wayne, there was a new Evangelical Mennonite Church less than a mile from our house where we joined a small study group and I taught a children's Sunday school class. In all three of these churches, we were regular choir members. Gradually, though, in Fort Wayne we realized that something was missing: We weren't hearing anything about working for peace other than through military service. We wanted our children to be taught at church as well as at home about non-violent resistance such as Jesus lived and taught.

Stan's mother knew that the Central District Conference, of which their family church was a part, wanted to plant a new General Conference church in Ft. Wayne. She told Stan, when we moved there, that we should consider helping with such a project.

A year or two later, when two representatives of a Church Planting Committee from First Mennonite Church in Berne, IN, stopped at the office where we worked and asked if we'd be interested in helping them plant a new church in Fort Wayne, we were already motivated and ready to be part of God's answer to their prayers as well as our own. The Berne church was a member of CDC, the same district conference as Stan's home church in Nappanee, IN.

The first gathering of what is now known as the Maplewood Mennonite Church was held in our small living room. It took only one meeting for us to realize that our house was too small for the new venture. For the first year, with leadership provided from Berne, we met for weekly bible study in the YWCA. Then the committee, with Stan's help as co-chair, located and purchased a parsonage with a long living-dining room large enough to double as a meeting place. Leonard Wiebe was just finishing seminary and he and his wife, Joan, were hired to provide pastoral leadership. They could have served well in a place that would have paid much better and provided much more security, but they felt the guiding hand of God and accepted this more challenging call. The Wiebes' outgoing personalities, firm commitment, and warm hospitality were just right for the growing suburbs. Two or three other families plus a couple of young professional Mennonite families who had moved to town were quickly involved in the life of our little house-church. We were amazed at how the Berne Church kept generously underwriting the budget in order to keep things moving ahead.

It was after the educational unit for a new church building had been completed that two of the professional couples accepted jobs which required them to relocate. Our little congregation began to dwindle, and we were all discouraged. So much to do, and so few people to carry on with the work! One night, Len and Joan invited Stan and me to the parsonage to talk things over. Pastor Len wondered aloud if we should just give up the effort. He didn't know what else to do.

With a passion that surprised even me, I blurted out my frustration: "You Mennonites don't *pray*." That statement was not really true, of course, but the prayers written for our worship services had always sounded pretty heady and formal to me. I'm certain that those prayers were politically and theologically proper, but my spirit had not been touched by them. (Let me hasten to say that this was undoubtedly my own problem –not everyone else's. As I reflect now on what probably seemed missing in the prayer life of the church at the time was a more mystical dependence upon the Holy Spirit –an open expectation of help from beyond our human endeavors.)

In response to my rudeness, Len looked me in the eye and said, "Well would you and Stan be willing to form a bible-study prayer group with Joan and me?"

Okay! So I had opened my mouth. It was time for me to back my words with action that could further facilitate my belief in God's availability to lead and give light to our path when we seek direction. We agreed to meet weekly around the table in our kitchen for bible study and prayer. We wanted to find our way together as young adults who wanted to serve God and see the church grow.

One area where I had lots of personal room to grow was trying to put my prayer thoughts into words. Having grown up with contemplative prayer, I found it very difficult to put my private and spontaneous conversation with God into suitable-sounding sentences and to pray them aloud. The very thought of vocal prayer filled me with complicating emotion.

The first time I was ever asked to pray aloud was at college. In the dining room at boarding school, the Quaker tradition of having a silent prayer of thanks was observed prior to meals, but at college the mealtime prayer was usually spoken or sung. Students who were involved in the spiritual life of the campus were often asked to offer a spoken mealtime prayer at lunch time on Thursdays. I always listened, impressed. In spite of the fact that I had a rich sense of communication with God, the possibility of being invited to pray aloud filled me with anxiety. How could I trust myself to put into words that very private part of my relationship with God? Surely words would fail me and emotion would overwhelm me.

The awful day came, as I was afraid it would, when I was asked to pray. I didn't want to admit how much I feared trying to do what I admired so much in others. Since I was being given a week's notice, I agreed to do it. I figured I'd try writing an acceptable prayer and memorize it in advance so I'd be completely prepared.

I cannot think of another time in my life when I promised to do something and then didn't. In fact, I completely forgot about my commitment until the next Thursday when the Dean of Women tapped the little bell at lunch time. Everyone was standing at their assigned tables. No one began to pray. That was unusual. And then it hit me! I was supposed to be praying. I broke out in a sweat. I had nothing prepared, and not one word would come to me. I wasn't about to do the obviously memorized "God is great, God is good" thing. That would be too childish. The silence seemed interminable. Finally, the dean tapped the bell again and we all sat down to eat. I tried to console myself with the truth that having a silent prayer was really my kind of prayer anyway, but I was embarrassed and I hated my inability to pray aloud.

The next time I got in touch with those feelings was while Stan and I were working in Indianapolis. We had been invited to help chaperone a group from the University of Illinois at the Flanner House Project. Fifteen students had come for the weekend to help paint renovated homes in a low-income section of the city. The local director of the project was a big, very outgoing, African-American. We were joking and having a wonderful time as the whole crew gathered around the table that first night. Then the director turned to me and said, "Bunnie, will you ask the blessing?" I nearly choked. In panic, but in the spirit of laughter, I quickly deferred, "Oh no, you go ahead." Stan and I have often laughed about that. Had he been the one the director asked to pray, we would have been okay.

There was yet another time that words failed me. It was when Stan and I were meeting with the Church Planting Committee in Berne. We'd finished lunch in the home of one of the committee members whose wife sometimes had heart-health problems, both physical and mental. The men wanted to show Stan some remodeling that had been done at their church and I agreed to stay with our hostess. Not long after the men left, the woman felt ill and asked me to help her get to the couch. She said she thought she might be dying, but she did not want me to call for help.

"Just pray," she said.

I was sitting beside her, holding her hand. I figured she meant that she wanted me to pray aloud and that she thought I could. I felt at a complete loss. I had no idea what to pray in that unusual situation. Even though I knew of her mental history, the two of us had met for the first time less than two hours earlier. I bowed my head and closed my eyes, still holding her hand, and prayed silently with an intensity born of dilemma, "God, help us both. Please give me appropriate words to pray if I need to pray aloud." No words came to my rescue. The silence seemed long but it probably wasn't. She started to get up saying that she was feeling better. She thanked me for praying and staying with her. Nevertheless, I felt like I had fallen short of what she expected.

I've learned that my felt inability is not entirely unique. Years later, as a pastor, I had just finished praying for one of our elderly saints in a nursing home when she said, "How I wish I could pray like that! I've just never been able to pray out loud." She went on to speculate. "Maybe it was because someone else always did it and I just didn't have to." She paused, reflecting. "There have been times when I would like to have prayed aloud with family members --but somehow I just couldn't do it."

Fortunately, in that little prayer group of four back in Fort Wayne, I found a way to get from "couldn't" to "could." Pastor Len called it conversational prayer. I'm not sure where he got the idea for that. We'd all been reading books by Elizabeth O'Connor from The Church of the Saviour in Washington, D.C., Catherine Marshall, Keith Miller, and Bruce Larson. Whatever they wrote, we read.

In conversational prayer, any or all members of the group contribute vocally to the prayer, adding a sentence or two at any point and as many different times as they have something they want to add. Silences between the various bits and pieces of the prayer were expected and quite okay. This made it much easier to participate prayerfully without having to struggle for words or think ahead to come up with a larger (more complete) prayer.

One morning, I sought to understand why vocal prayer and/or meaningful writing about spiritual things seemed so hard for me. I realized that in spite of the fact that I loved words, my prayer life –indeed my intimate spiritual life-- existed in a dimension that was beyond the busyness and adequacy of words.

Conversational prayer gave me a handle that allowed me to try speaking from the heart about things that deeply mattered to me and got me beyond the fear of expressing myself inadequately or poorly. It occurred to me that if this sort of prayer was helping me to grow in my ability to share more openly in a faith community, it might be a good way to help our children express themselves beyond the rote prayers I had taught them. We explained that instead of just reading the prayers from the devotional materials we used, we could create our own "family prayer" together. They were not at all hesitant to participate.

At this point, I need to explain that my brother, Don, and his family lived near us in Ft. Wayne. Stan's brother, Lew, and his wife had just visited us to say goodbye before leaving for a three-year voluntary service assignment in Tanzania with Mennonite Central Committee's Teachers Abroad Program.

Almost as soon as we started the prayer that first morning, eight-year-old Kim spoke up: "Dear God, please help Uncle Lew as he goes to teach in Africa." Then four-year-old Jeff quickly added, "And help Uncle Don stay at home." We've smiled often about Jeff's earnest plea. (Okay! So we've chuckled about that. It was funny.)

In order to help focus my naturally right brained and contemplatively trained thinking, I began praying aloud when I was alone in private devotion. Sometimes it helped to structure my running conversation with God if I knelt to pray. The kneeling gave an intentional beginning and ending to formal prayer, and speaking aloud helped me get my thoughts in oral order. But my heart and mind carried prayer thoughts throughout the day --thoughts directed to God and thoughts reminding me to listen for what God might want to say to me.

Pray without ceasing.

I Thessalonians 5: 17 KJV

Len, Joan, Stan, and I grew in spiritual community as we studied, talked, and prayed together. Why were we all happily amazed when several families from a more conservative Mennonite church came to visit our dwindling congregation and found it to be exactly the sort of place they had been hoping to find as a new church home? These were people who shared most of the same values and who were far more financially able than any of us who had ventured out to build a new congregation. Without exception all those families were quite successful in businesses of their own and were generous contributors to the work of God's kingdom here on earth.

Questions for Individual Reflection or Group Sharing

1. Have you ever been in a situation where "what you feel is right" is compromised? What did you do about it?

2. Does the pursuit of prestige or extra money ever present a temptation?

3. How has the call to faithful living drawn you to serve and pray with others? Are there stories you can share?

4. Are you comfortable praying aloud in a public or family setting? If so, share how you learned to do that.

5. Are you or have you ever been part of a sharing group where you and others could speak openly and freely about spiritual concerns?

chapter 5

Prayer for Personal and Practical Connections

This first story is about how prayer, plus the support of my prayer group, helped me make a long-awaited connection. We had received word that my dad's father was dying.

Grandpa Bundy, as I mentioned in an earlier chapter, was my earthly substitute for a father after Dad left us and moved to Cadiz --the town where he and Grandpa had the office for their Bundy's Moving and Transfer business. Grandpa and Grandma lived just down the road from us while I was growing up, and although Dad lived only a half-hour away, we saw him only about once a year when Mother would send us to visit him on a Sunday afternoon or evening. She wanted us to know each other, but our quickie visits never lasted more than half an hour or so. Dad's new wife did not like for him to be reminded of us and never permitted him to visit us.

While I hardly knew Dad, Grandpa and I were the best of friends. He never seemed to tire of having me around. Some of my favorite memories had to do with his letting me help him at home count the weekly change from their business and package it in paper rolls to take to the bank on Monday mornings. He also kept cartons of Clark, O Henry, and Baby Ruth candy bars handy which helped nourish our already sweet relationship. Even after I was married, I always greeted him and left him with hugs. When I turned sixteen, he was the one who taught me to drive –risking his life and his new Packard. He called me his little girl and I knew that in his heart was a place I'd always belong. But we had ***never*** discussed matters of faith. In my eyes, Grandpa was a good man; he just wasn't very openly religious. He regularly went to meeting, but I never heard him speak about God.

Of course, I saw him much less after I went away to boarding school and college. And adding to the distance between us after I was married, Dad, his wife Lois, Grandma and Grandpa moved to California where they purchased houses across the street from each other in Pasadena. Being that far away and now that my siblings and I were grown and on our own, Lois felt less threatened, and she permitted Dad to extend an open invitation for us to visit them and my grandparents.

It took a few years for us to even consider that financially, but eventually we established a vacation fund and planned to drive across country during the summer between our daughter's 2nd and 3rd grade school year.

At Christmastime we received word that Grandpa was not at all well and probably would not live until summer. I felt an urgency to see him again and talk with him before he died. Mother had long ago told me that Grandpa blamed himself for Dad's philandering. To make a long story short Grandpa had earlier had another woman too. He was seldom available when Grandma needed him to help out with their eight growing children. It was not until Dad got involved with Lois that Grandpa saw the impact of his example and he did a complete turn-around. Mother told us that Grandma had benefited greatly as a result Grandpa's remorse.

Mother was glad for Grandma, of course, but it didn't ease her own pain. Dad did not turn around. Grandpa spoke to Mother more than once about the guilt he bore regarding our family's plight, but he never talked with me or others about it. If, indeed, he was still carrying that burden, I wanted to help set him free before he died.

We made immediate plans to fly to California. By this time, Lois was providing meals and daily household help for Grandpa and Grandma. I told my prayer group about the conversation I wanted to have with Grandpa and asked them to support me in prayer while we were gone.

Dad was eager to show my family all the exciting tourist sites in their area. He took us to see Hollywood movie sets, the street of stars, and he pointed out the homes of famous people. One day we watched floats being made for the Rose Parade and visited the Rose Bowl stadium. On New Year's Day he took us to the big parade in all its floral and royal glory. We were seeing Grandpa and Grandma at the beginning or ending of each exciting day as well.

In the wee morning hours of our last full vacation day, I awakened and realized that I'd been so wrapped up in wonderful activity (and was so tired at the end of each day) that I hadn't found time to have my private talk with Grandpa. Worse than that, I'd forgotten to keep praying about it. I could hardly believe that I had been so distracted by getting to know Dad, and having him be with my little family, that I'd neglected the most important reason why we'd made the trip earlier than previously planned. I remembered my support group back home and took some comfort in the fact that they were probably being more faithful than I. I asked God to open a way for me to reach Grandpa's heart. I knew I was going to have to be alert to an "open door" because Dad had a full day planned for us at Knott's Berry Farm.

When we got up that morning, Lois informed us that Grandpa was feeling less well than usual and planned just to stay in bed all day. There was my "in." I went to his room, cheerily kissed his forehead, took his hand and knelt beside his bed so we could talk face to face. After a bit of small talk, I told him that Mother had told me about his sense of responsibility for our broken family. I wish I could recall and record the actual conversation that we had, but I will always remember and cherish the feelings that accompanied the words. I know that this visit was about forgiveness and God's grace. I also thanked him for playing such an important role in my life. Tears washed both his eyes and mine. Still on my knees, I prayed briefly aloud –straight from the heart. Dad called from the kitchen asking if I was ready to leave for the Berry Farm. –And we were on our way.

When we returned that evening, the first words out of Lois's mouth were, "Ruth, what on earth did you say to your Grandpa this morning? After you left, he got out of bed, got dressed and went to mid-week meeting." Clearly, she was astonished by what had happened. Her question, however, appeared to be rhetorical and I didn't need to answer. I felt that Grandpa had been reconnected in a new and freeing way with his Creator. He surprised us all by living for several years after that.

The following stories are about what I call "ironing board prayers."

Everyone did a lot more ironing back in the 1960's. I used to do much more ironing than I did before "wash and wear" fabrics significantly reduced our ironing time. I enjoyed the clean work of ironing and often used the time for prayer. Sometimes those prayers were for or about current concerns and the need for wisdom beyond my own. Often they were for or about family members whose piece of clothing I was ironing at the time –sometimes just unspoken prayers of gratitude. God hears the contemplative prayers of our hearts as well as our words.

The following poem playfully illustrates gratitude for love and practical connection:

Laundry Room Passion

Ironing shirts is such a clean, sweet-scented job!
Smoothing each crisp collar and cuff, I breathe deeply
of the man I married and remember how hard I worked
to perfect this household chore --this one task
that invites me to straighten out the wrinkles I observe
and restore the freshness that first attracted me and others
to this clean-cut college man who needed a woman
such as I to keep him well-groomed and going –with me.

Occasionally, even yet as I straighten out the sleeves
and carefully iron the plackets and pleats, I imagine
them filled with skin, muscle, and bone –his of course--
arms wrapped tightly around me, holding me close, his cheek
next to mine, nose turned to my ear and my own perfume.
How could any wife, still young at heart, buy only
"wash and wear" and deprive herself the home-made romance,
the laundry soap-opera, of ironing her husband's shirts?

At another point in my life, I was concerned about a broken relationship with a former co-worker, and that concern entered my prayer-time one day while ironing. I asked God for wisdom and guidance that could open dialogue for mutual forgiveness and reconnection. Just moments later I was amazed to remember that she and her husband would soon be celebrating a wedding anniversary. "*Why not get the nicest card available and send them good wishes? Don't say anything more; just wish them a happy anniversary.*" The message was clear. I did as the still small voice inside directed.

A few months later, this couple came for a visit and they mentioned the anniversary card I'd sent. We were able to forgive each other and let bygones be bygones. It was the weekend that churches everywhere were celebrating World Wide Communion. Never before and probably never since has communion been such a profound spiritual experience for me. My own world was again truly at peace with God.

There was yet another time that I received clear direction while ironing.

One of the new members of our church joined our prayer group. He was a builder who was known for his quality construction. My husband had always dreamed of designing and helping to build a home for our family. We liked Fort Wayne and were thoroughly entrenched in the life of the church.

There were new housing developments around the church and within five minutes of Stan's office. This seemed like a good time to proceed. We knew we could trust the builder to help us consider what we could afford, critique Stan's design, and build it for us. He allowed Stan and me to help when and where we could, such as painting the rooms and finishing all the woodwork and doors. We watched and worked as our dream became a reality.

But when we'd been in our brand-new house for only a month or so, the telephone stopped working. The line was dead. Repairmen from the telephone company came out and spent a long time checking everything they could think of. All seemed to be as it should be except that the line was dead. They went home baffled. A special crew of troubleshooters arrived the next day. They double-checked the entry line and every phone jack in the house. The supervisor came into the family room where I was ironing and just shook his head.

"The phones and everything else seem to be in tip-top order," he reported. "I simply don't understand why the line is dead."

I could see both confusion and compassion in his eyes as he continued. "There's only one more thing we can explore. We'll have to cut through your flooring and into the concrete slab where the telephone lines are buried."

I was immediately ready to argue, "Surely you don't need to cut into my inlaid linoleum! It's brand new." The men were as troubled as I was or perhaps even more so. After all, they understood how telephone lines work. I didn't. They were professional technicians. I wasn't. I didn't expect to know how to fix the system. They were supposed to know, but. . .. The supervisor turned away reluctantly. He understood my dismay both at having no phone service and at the prospect of what was ahead. "We'll be back in the morning to begin," he said.

There were dollar signs in my mind, additional costs that we couldn't afford, and besides that I was afraid my floor would never look really nice again. I kept on ironing and again used that clean, quiet work time to pray. "*God, please help those men to find what is causing the problem and fix it without having to tear up our house.*" After many more strokes of the iron, one of those answering lights went on in my head.

I recalled my lying in the hammock on the back patio earlier in the week when it started to rain. I had noticed some thin wires sticking out of a little hole in the aluminum siding. It occurred to me that it might not be good for them to get wet, so I gently pushed them back inside the hole where they'd be protected. I remembered that Stan had planned to someday put a telephone jack on the patio. I wondered if those wires could have gotten wet in spite of my effort to keep them dry.

I don't know how to describe the difference between casual thought and illuminated thought, but this seemed special. I thought that this memory just might be part of the answer to my prayer.

When the men returned with their tools the next morning to cut through the floor, I told them about the little hole out back and the wires. "Could they have gotten wet and shorted out?" The men raced to the patio, retrieved and separated the perfectly dry wires, wrapped each one in black electrical tape and the problem was solved. What a relief --for them and for me! I learned that I had grounded the phone lines by inadvertently pushing these two unwrapped wires together as I was trying to avert trouble from the rain. Thank goodness God could speak to me in spite of my ignorance so that the problem could be solved and our phone service re-connected.

Just as our thoughts can be guided to find solutions for broken relationships, prayer can help us solve other mysteries as well.

Questions for Individual Reflection and or Group Sharing

1. Have you ever felt a responsibility to share your faith with a family member or friend who might need a new vision of the forgiveness and grace that God provides?

2. Do you believe that God knows our thoughts and hears the wordless prayers that I have called "prayers of the heart"?

3. Do you have a story about a relationship that was broken and has since been healed –or is still in need of healing.

4. If we believe that God intends for us to live at peace with others in our families, communities, and world, are there practical ways that we can facilitate loving connections?

5. Do you ever pray about practical household matters when you need wisdom beyond your own knowledge or understanding? Have you a story to share –maybe even about help to find a lost item?

chapter 6

Opening to a Fuller Life

Our study-prayer group at church in Ft. Wayne was noting the charismatic movement of the 1960's. The hippies and God-seekers of that day were giving a lot of attention to spiritual gifts and manifestations of the Holy Spirit in one's life. One of the manifestations that seemed strangest to me was speaking in tongues. I'd only *heard about* such things. I'd never been in a setting where that happened. I was curious, but frankly, it seemed a little weird to me and I wasn't sure I could handle something like that. I would prefer some more useful gift –perhaps the ability to heal. Much as I didn't want to resist anything that God had for me, I found it hard to be open to speaking in tongues.

Pentecostal writers such as David duPlessis and some other preachers and writers were saying that all people who were baptized by the Holy Spirit would speak in tongues. Others were skeptical about such a broad statement. As a birthright Quaker, I believed that I had been baptized by the Holy Spirit when, as a teenager, I had made a conscious decision to be a follower of Jesus Christ, but now Christians from other denominations and popular writers were speaking about "something more" and a "second baptism."

It was with openness of spirit that I had read all of the books Catherine Marshall had written up to that time. Other books that had captured my spiritual attention were *A Testament of Devotion* by Thomas R. Kelly, *The Whole Person in a Broken World* by Paul Tournier, *The Taste of New* Wine and *A Second Touch* by Keith Miller.

I was trying to understand new dimensions of healing during this time too --particularly as it related to the hurt in my heart that periodically surfaced as a result of Dad's leaving when I was a child. I also wanted inner affirmation that my spiritual commitment was complete so God could use me fully and effectively. I wanted to know that my motives were pure. This is one of my prayers that spilled out on paper in July of 1967.

Prayer for Life

God:
Awaken my awareness
to the living gift
within myself.
The gift
that is meant to be
my service to humankind--
to my world.
Help me discover
the talent you created,
that is waiting to be enhanced
by your Spirit.
Grant, God,
deeper understanding.
I am eager
to live more fully.
Fill me with more of your love--
I need to care for others
more deeply.

Forgive my base desire
to live selfishly,
to aim for status
and personal gain.
Sharpen my sense
of your plan and your power
that I may resist
temptation.
Teach me more
of courage and faith
that I may walk
in greater obedience.
God:
Strengthen my belief
in the availability
of your Spirit--
That my life
and your purpose
can merge
in fulfillment.

For several years, I had used and been influenced by the devotional books of E. Stanley Jones, a Methodist missionary to India and a prolific writer. Dr. Paul Shelly, the bible professor for whom I worked my first two years at college, gave me the one that got me started titled *Growing Spiritually*. I purchased and read several more of his books after that.

E. Stanley Jones taught that speaking in tongues was just one sign of the Holy Spirit in a person's life –that some people, but certainly not all would be given that gift.

First Mennonite Church in Berne, IN, sponsor of our church plant in Ft. Wayne, kept in touch and frequently invited our Maplewood members to special programs. One of their missionaries, Gerald Stucky, was home on furlough from Columbia, South America. Gerald and his wife had met David duPlessis in Columbia where he was teaching that the gift of tongues <u>always</u> accompanied the baptism of the Spirit, and the Stuckys were given that gift. Since there seemed to be a growing interest in the charismatic movement, Gerald invited David duPlessis to speak at the Berne church. We at Maplewood were invited to hear him as well. It was an opportunity to see and hear this man in person, but I was torn about whether or not to attend. I wanted to. I didn't want to. I thought my Christian commitment was valid, but what if duPlessis's guaranteed proof didn't come? What if it did?

I'd read a lot about that gift, absolutely dreaded the possibility that I might be given it, and then moved on to the place where, if that were the gift God had for me, I'd try to receive it willingly if not enthusiastically.

E. Stanley Jones had even warned in his writings about groups who expected that gift to always accompany the baptism of the Holy Spirit. He said it was a mistake to use one particular gift as a measure of true spirituality.

I was standing at the bottom of the stairs in our new house deciding whether or not to change my clothes and join those who planned to attend that meeting with duPlessis. I was at zero hour. If I was going to go, I needed to get a move on.

Just then the doorbell rang. It was a lady from the drapery shop. She had come to measure the windows in our new house. I breathed a prayer of relief. My decision was made. I couldn't leave.

Not long after that, our pastor got the surprising word that E. Stanley Jones was in the States and was leading an ashram at Lake St. Mary's in Ohio. Pastor Wiebe invited a member of our congregation who was a native of India and me to drive out with him for a day at that ashram. I was excited! There was absolutely no question about my wanting to go.

Since there would be open time during the afternoon, I took along the book I was reading at the time. It was Catherine Marshall's *Beyond Ourselves*, which drew heavily on *A Christian's Secret of a Happy Life* written long ago by a Quaker woman, Hannah Whitall Smith. I was just ready to read the chapter about receiving the Holy Spirit. I was eager to find a shade tree and drink in her message while we waited for the evening service.

We had no sooner arrived at the campgrounds than Pastor Wiebe turned to me and said, "Ruth, it's such a lovely day! What say we take a walk together around the campground?" Had our pastor not been so spiritually attractive to me at that point in my life, I might well have taken the walk with him. The invitation was perfectly innocent on his part –perhaps he even wanted to converse further about things we'd discussed in the study-prayer group, but I immediately recognized that invitation as a temptation I needed to avoid if indeed I meant business with God that day. I chose the tree and the book.

I went to the evening service feeling intensely eager to hear whatever E. Stanley Jones had to say. Even though his topic had not been advertised or even previously announced, it was like he was telling me something I already knew when he said at the beginning of the service: "I've decided to speak about the baptism of the Holy Spirit this evening."

While altar calls had always seemed foreign to me, I knew that if he gave an invitation to come forward that night for the laying on of hands and opening one's life to a fuller measure of the Holy Spirit, there was nothing that would keep me from going forward. Not even the fact that I saw two Bluffton College professors and their wives in attendance as well. Not even the possibility of speaking in tongues. I wanted to receive whatever

God had for me. The "altar" in that lakeside pavilion was a row of slightly rusty folding chairs. I was one of at least a dozen folks who went forward to receive whatever special blessing God had for us. I confess that I hoped for at least a special little tingle of affirmation as E. Stanley Jones laid his hands on my head and prayed; however, I didn't feel a thing that seemed unusual.

Conversation was lively in the car on the way home. So lively in fact that Pastor Wiebe turned the wrong way and we were on the outskirts of Columbus, OH, before anyone noticed. A quick stop allowed for a call that would notify our spouses that we'd be considerably later getting home than we'd planned.

Even as we talked, I wondered if anything truly had changed as a result of that day. I still wasn't sure, but I'd been open and obedient to the best that I knew. The next day, I felt completely at peace and knew that I'd done all I could to commit myself and my life completely to God. I wondered if Stan would understand if I told him what had or had not happened. Should I keep this a secret between me and God?

Because I didn't want to keep secrets from my husband, I told him. Even though he is not as mystically inclined as I, he wasn't put off by my spiritual search and commitment. In ensuing days, I realized that I knew a new lightness of heart that would allow me to quit seeking some obvious gift of the spirit. I was at peace.

Little did I know then just how I would come to recognize that fuller measure of the Spirit in my life. (More on that in another chapter.)

While our family was still living in Fort Wayne and enjoying the new house we'd helped to build, Stan realized that his job dissatisfaction was growing more pronounced. If he wanted something more satisfying, he realized he needed to look elsewhere.

I loved being a full-time homemaker but also realized that I wanted "something more" than just our perfect little family of four and the attainment of our dream home. We didn't have money for me to complete work for my college degree; so, we began thinking about something else that would be more soul-satisfying --maybe service in some needier part of the world.

I filled out an application for the Peace Corps and also sent letters of inquiry to American Friends Service Committee and Mennonite Central Committee regarding possible service assignments. If we took a two- or three-year voluntary service assignment overseas, we could try to find renters and use the rent to make mortgage payments while we were gone. We were not thinking of making a permanent move.

While waiting for responses to inquiries about voluntary service, something quite unexpected happened. In the middle of a routine afternoon of work at Stan's office, he telephoned me to ask a crazy question.

"How would you like to move back to Bluffton?"

"Bluffton?" I echoed in disbelief. "I wouldn't."

That was not the sort of thing either of us had in mind. Stan talked on: "Harry Yoder was just here. He's the current Director of Development at the College, and he said that they are looking for a Director of Financial Aid who would also work part-time with him in development. He wondered if I might be interested in applying for the position."

Stan had always been staunchly loyal to his alma mater, but neither of us had ever dreamed of going back to Bluffton to live. That small town compared to Ft. Wayne didn't seem to have much to offer.

"One thing," Stan continued, "Harry said you could go back to school tuition-free if I worked there."

Oh my goodness! "Well! Now *THAT* has possibilities," I said. "Think about it and we can talk when I get home," he said. I *REALLY* wanted to finish work toward a college degree. (I'll eventually tell about how I had been saving small bits of personal income toward that end –but not here.)

I had just finished my sophomore year when Stan graduated. We got married and I joined him in alternative service. I still had two more years to go for my B.A.

After hanging up the phone, reality began to set in. I was eager for Stan to get home so we could talk through the ramifications of a move like that.

The pay at a church college would be nothing to write home about, but after all, this was a service-oriented option for Stan. We were totally ripe for a possibility like this. The fact that I could pick up my college work without losing any already earned credits was better than anything I'd ever thought possible. It had been about thirteen years since I'd been in college; our children were both in school now, and I was ready for a new challenge. The more Stan and I considered this invitation, the more it seemed like God's new direction for us. I remembered again the Scripture:

> ***Trust in the Lord with all your heart and lean not on your own understanding; In all your ways acknowledge him, and he will make your paths straight.***
>
> **--Proverbs 3:5-6. NIV**

Some time ago when I was participating in a workshop on prayer, someone asked whether we can ever be *sure* of God guidance in our lives. The result of our discussion was that it is usually in retrospect that one can be most certain. Thomas Merton said it this way: "Looking for God in prayer is like looking for a path in a field of untrodden snow. Walk across the snow and there is your path."

There was no doubt in my mind about God's guidance when

I headed to Bluffton College the first time. Miss Edna Ramseyer, the Dean of Women who kept tabs on campus romances, told me she thought I might look back someday and think God led me to Bluffton so I could meet Stan. I remember taking that a bit lightly when she said it, but then who knows?

Dr. Paul R. Shelly, Head of the Bible Department, the professor who first called on me after I wrote to Bluffton for admission information, and the one for whom I worked after classes every Monday through Friday, gave Stan and me a copy of the book *Christ and the Fine Arts* for a wedding gift. Inside, he had written:

To Ruth and Stan

Best wishes for a happy and useful life,

Paul R. Shelly.

Psalm 37:5

At various transitional points in my life, I've gone back to that inscription believing that the Scripture reference was there for a purpose.

The mysterious movement of cloud and fire now seemed to be leading us back to Bluffton. For Stan, the potential change offered a more meaningful sort of servanthood. For me, it offered the fulfillment of a dream for more education. None of our family or friends (not even our small-group) knew that we'd been hoping and praying for a new opportunity to serve and grow. The offer had come "out of the blue."

This new opportunity felt like a continuation of God's provision in my life, and it seemed a perfect fit for Stan to work in a place he loved. We didn't see this as a two or three-year voluntary service assignment so we had to make some sacrifices.

A year earlier, we'd built the home where we thought we'd probably spend the rest of our lives. Moving meant we'd have to sell our comfortable new house. The housing market in Fort Wayne was glutted and we knew we'd have trouble selling a year-old house for what we actually had invested in it. Much less could we expect to be paid for our sweat equity –finishing all the woodwork, painting etc. ourselves. In order to sell our house at actual cost and save realtor fees, we put a "**For Sale by Owner**" sign in the yard.

The housing market in small-town Bluffton was tight and prices were considerably higher whenever an occasional house came up for sale or rent. We agreed that Stan would live in Bluffton during the week and just come home on weekends until we could sell our house and find something affordable to either start buying or to rent in Bluffton.

Questions for Individual Reflection and or Group Sharing

1. What nudges toward change or growing commitment have you felt in your life?

2. Have you ever worried about what might be asked of you if you committed your life <u>fully</u> to God?

3. Share stories of God's leading or of specific answers to prayer in your own life or the life of your family or friends? Do you find it hard to talk about such things?

4. What is the desire of your heart today?

5. What books or writers have been a spiritual inspiration for you?

chapter 7

Dealing with Conscience and Fear

As a child, I was taught that all people, regardless of color, were equal. There were some students of African descent in the Mt. Pleasant public-school system, but never more than two or three at one time in my classes. As stated earlier, I considered one of them a very good friend.

There was a Native American family who lived about a mile from us. Mother sometimes hired the father or his bright teenage sons to help with heavy chores or repairs that required some expertise. We liked and respected that family a lot.

At boarding school, there were a few students from foreign countries. I particularly remember students from Japan and the Netherlands. When I was elected Girls' Director of our Student Government Association, the elected Boys' Director was an African American. We worked well together.

After being accepted at Bluffton College, I was put in touch with a Mennonite from Pennsylvania who was to be my roommate. We corresponded immediately and were looking forward to sharing a room. But a week before the beginning of the school year, I received a telegram from Dr. Shelly asking if I would be willing to room with a Puerto Rican? "Reply just YES or NO. No explanation needed." Obviously, he was working with an issue of race. There was no way I could have conscientiously said NO in spite of the fact that the previous assignment had seemed ideal.

My Puerto Rican roommate and I got along just fine even though she made closer friends with those who didn't work every day after classes as I did. Her work assignment was in the kitchen before breakfast and before I was out of bed.

Though I was not aware of any interracial dating on campus in the early Fifties, there were many interracial friendships. A football teammate of Stan's whom I particularly admired wrote in my yearbook, addressing me with my nickname. And then he signed it with his nickname.

> *Bunnie:*
>
> *Being your friend has been an honor and a pleasure.*
>
> *Best of everything to you and yours.*
>
> *-- Ollie*

Because of those good relationships in the past, my concern was heightened regarding racial prejudice and the injustices people of color had to endure.

In the late 1960's when Stan and I were living in Fort Wayne, racial tensions were running high all over our country. Our city was no exception. These were the days leading up to Martin Luther King's assassination. Crosses were being burned on the lawns of people who risked integrating neighborhoods. It was a frightening time.

We had taken an unpopular stand when we were ready to sell our first home and move to the one we had just built in a development a few miles closer to our church. The realtor asked us, apparently as a matter of routine, to sign a paper saying that we would not allow him to show our house to people of color. I told him that we couldn't conscientiously do that because we believe in equal opportunity. He was not at all pleased but, after some serious discussion, he realized that we were not going to change our minds. As he gathered up his papers to leave, he mumbled in a lowered voice, "Well I hope nobody asks to see proof." In spite of our willingness to sell to African Americans, he brought only Caucasians to see our house and it was sold in a timely manner.

We certainly didn't expect to have another house to sell so soon, but a little more than a year later, the issue of neighborhood integration was again in the forefront of our concerns as we prepared to move back to Bluffton. A cross had been burned in the development next to ours. One of the advantages we saw in trying to sell the house ourselves was that we could show it to anyone who wanted to see it.

I was a member of Churchwomen for Change and Reconciliation, a racially and religiously mixed organization. At one of the programs, I'd heard a panelist tell about her family's experience trying to get realtors to show them homes in the new housing developments north of the city. "They say they can't show us homes in those neighborhoods because Whites won't allow it," she reported. The woman's husband was a professional man and they could obviously afford a nice home.

Stan and I discussed the possibility of my showing our new house to them, but I had to admit how frightening it would be for me to be alone with the children while he was in Bluffton if we were to awaken some night to loud voices and a cross burning in our yard. On the other hand I believed that justice was at stake, and I knew that it called for people of courage to risk the animosity and actions of those who disagreed --including the Ku Klux Klan.

It was generally believed that integration would reduce the

value of surrounding properties. I hated the thought of causing my neighbors financial or emotional distress; however, my conscience kept reminding me that we should be involved in social change. I admitted to my prayer group that I would prefer to have people of color move in as one of my neighbors so I could help welcome them instead of merely selling and then moving away. In prayer I also confessed my fear of retaliation and prayed for wisdom and strength to do what was right in spite of my fear for the welfare of our children.

I called the panelist and told her we had a house for sale in the Oakhurst subdivision and if she and her husband wanted to see it, I would be glad to show it to them. When their big white Cadillac came into our driveway, I suspected that the house and neighborhood was more modest than what they really wanted. Indeed, I was right. They said they appreciated my showing the house to them, but they really were looking for something larger. I was glad that I'd had the courage to give them the opportunity to buy it.

Week after week went by. No one seemed interested in our Ft. Wayne house and there was nothing available to buy in Bluffton. The fall semester was nearly over and we wondered if buyers were skeptical about the "For Sale by Owner" sign in the yard of such a new house in a new development. Perhaps they thought something was wrong with the house.

As a statement of faith for my own benefit, I paraphrased the 23rd Psalm in one of my devotional times:

The Lord Is My Realtor

I shall not worry.
He makes me rest
in quiet confidence.
He leads me in peaceful
assurance.
He restores my soul.
He leads us in paths
of goodness and purpose
for His name's sake.
Even though I walk through
streets with no vacancies
I fear no evil
for He is directing.
His unlimited wisdom
comforts me.
He prepares a home
before us
in the presence of our need.
He anoints our lives
with good things.
My gratitude overflows.
Surely goodness and mercy
shall follow us
all the days of our lives.
And we shall dwell
in God's Kingdom
forever.

Eventually, a small rental on the edge of Bluffton's campus became available. God's pillar of cloud and fire was moving again. Because I wanted to get started in classes at the beginning of the second semester, we employed our same real estate company and added the sales commission to our asking price. Again, we refused to sign papers designed to block the integration of neighborhoods. Two weeks later, the house was sold to a Caucasian family for our asking price.

Questions for Individual Reflection and or Group Sharing

1. Have you ever needed to take an unpopular stand based on what you believe?
   If so, are you willing to share more about that?

2. How do you seek courage to help you face fear? Does it help?

3. What are the important social issues facing the church or culture today?

4. Have you felt called to work for justice in some particular way? How and when?

chapter 8

Our World Falls Apart – Dealing with Pain and Questions

Our new life in Bluffton seemed to be going well. The children adjusted quickly. We still were a one-car family, but that was no problem. A school bus took Kim from our front door on Spring Street to the middle school in Beaverdam. Jeff could easily walk the one block to Bluffton's elementary school. Our little white bungalow was right on the edge of campus. Stan could walk to his office and I could walk to classes. We quickly became involved in First Mennonite Church which was on Jackson Street --directly across from the elementary school. I enjoyed being back in college and I loved caring for my family as well.

News reports and forums on campus, though, were laden with stories of cultural challenge and upheaval, all typical of the 1960's. It seemed that the world around us was falling apart –morally at least. Perhaps it was only natural that what I was observing and learning about would become the subject of a poem.

"Christmas 1969" was written in early December, and although I was certain it would be too late for the Christmas issue of *The Mennonite,* I sent it anyway. The editor must have liked it well enough to do some juggling because it appeared in the December 22 issue.

Christmas 1969

The star softly haloed
    with golden light
Is largely unseen
    in a neon night.
Color bulbs flashing
    around us
Blind would-be-eyes
    to a Bethlehem view.

The angels' song—
    hope and joy
Is drowned in the big
    top-ten of despair.
Spotlights, attained,
    cast empty shadows
And grasped-at-glitter
    does not go around.

Shepherds? Ho-hum,
    irrelevant, passé,
Angels? Delusion—
    hallucination, we'd say.
A star? Perhaps. . .
    Moon is ours; Mars is next.
Wise men? Of course!
    We write the text.

Noisy gongs,
    clanging cymbals:
Dig the beat, man,
    knowledge and pot.

Joy to the world
    hey nonny nonny—
Christ is born
    and a big, "So what?"

Shortly after I wrote and submitted that poem, our personal world fell apart. Although I was completely unaware of the chaos that would soon envelop my family, the poem's cynical tone probably matched one or two of my worst moments in the days and weeks ahead.

Here's our story:

Stan came home early on the Friday afternoon just a few days before Christmas, threw his coat on the couch, and said, "Say hello to the second ________!" He named a neighbor who had been head of the college food service department until he had been recently let go. At practically the same time, that family had been saddled with unexpected hospital and medical bills as a result of their newborn child's physical abnormalities. I was so touched by the pain I knew they must be feeling that I had taken a collection among neighbors and co-workers to show love and support. We wanted them to know we wished them well as they were preparing to move to another state.

Though Stan's termination came as a complete surprise to me, he didn't have to tell me what he meant by referring to our neighbor that Friday afternoon. The look on his face said it all. He was struggling to believe it. I couldn't believe it! It was too devastating to even imagine. Stan gave a brief description of what had just happened then turned and moved heavily toward the door saying, "I've got to go for a walk and get some fresh air."

I hurried to our bedroom, tears flooding my eyes. "God," I cried aloud in agony, "If you've ever helped me, you've got to help me now." Aimlessly I reached for Kleenex and ***The Living New***

Testament: Paraphrased on my dresser. It seemed ridiculous to think the bible could speak to this. I couldn't think of any biblical stories about someone being fired. But where else could I turn? The book flopped open as I put it on the bed and fell to my knees in front of it. My eyes were flooded with tears. I couldn't see to read.

I believed that God had led us back to Bluffton! How could something like this be happening? What did Stan do or not do that caused him to be fired? Is my husband not the person I thought he was? To me, being fired from a job meant serious failure. In the 1950's and 60's it was common for men to work a lifetime for the same company. In more recent years, being "let go" is much more common for economic reasons in the state or nation, and it does not carry the kind of disgrace I felt when this happened in our family.

I was awash in shame that horrible afternoon. It wasn't in my nature to accuse my husband, but my confused mind struggled with terrible scenarios. It also was not in my nature at the time to question authority figures that I also knew and thought I could trust.

There had been scandal in Bluffton a few weeks earlier when the public-school treasurer was fired for embezzlement. Did the College think Stan had embezzled money from financial aid accounts? Will everyone we know think that of Stan? What WILL everyone think –especially when even I don't know what to think other than that Stan must be guilty of something terribly wrong? My own confidence in him had received a severe blow, but like it or not we were in it together.

Still on my knees and with sobbing subsiding, I lifted my head to wipe away tears, blow my nose and try to get a grip on myself. Words from the open bible on the bed before me grabbed my attention --the print seemed larger and bolder than all the surrounding verses:

> ***Now it is time to forgive him and comfort him. Otherwise he may become so bitter and discouraged that he won't be able to recover. Please show him now that you still do love him very much.***
>
> **-- II Corinthians 2:7-8**

Immediately I realized that if anyone in the world was hurting more than I that afternoon, it had to be Stan. I knew what I had to do. I recognized it as God's immediate and clear direction for me. I had thought help from Scripture for a situation such as this was unavailable. In that moment, I didn't care about biblical context, but checking later I saw that the passage was Paul's instruction regarding an issue in the church at Corinth, but I also knew with certainty that this was God's message for me in our devastating situation. I read those words again and again in the agonizing days and weeks ahead. God wasn't cheering me up. This was an *assignment* –something to ***do.*** Something that made sense. It took the spotlight off my hurting heart and focused it on Stan's. It wasn't what I might have expected, but it was what I needed. Isn't this what the marriage covenant is all about --standing by one another in the bad times as well as the good? A few months later in a creative writing class I reflected in a poem.

This is Forever

The promise was made
On a wild flower day while
Breathing April hours,

Clutching tender hopes
That Now would last
Forever.

But when darkness came
A tear-soaked pillow
Stifled dreams
And whispered nightmares
Until the dawn. It seemed
Forever.

The adult morning
Brought a fragrant bouquet:
Love shares
All of life's hours.
So shall it be
Forever.

Stan had waited until after 5:00, when his office staff would have gone home, in order to clean out his desk and pick up his personal belongings, but he discovered that the lock on his office door had been changed and he couldn't get in. To his already damaged sense of self this added another blow. Obviously, they didn't trust him. How else could he/we interpret that?

I needed to be studying for mid-term exams but I simply could not concentrate. I didn't want to live.

I remember walking around campus alone in the dark that night trying to sort things out. Stopping in the parking lot behind College Hall I prayed for the welfare of the college. Through tears I also prayed for God to bless and help both Stan and the man who fired him.

(*Reflecting on that night sometime later, I was reminded of the evening at Lake St. Mary's when I prayed sincerely and expectantly to be filled with the Holy Spirit --yet felt no special change. In retrospect, I realized that my prayer in the face of our current circumstance would undoubtedly have been different if it were not for that previous special time of total dedication to a grace-filled Christ.*)

We forced ourselves to go to church as usual on Sunday. A young professor, who was a member of our church and who was working with Stan on a campus committee, saw Stan as we arrived and asked him something about a meeting which was scheduled for the next day. Stan had to tell him that he wouldn't be there because he was no longer an employee. The professor was shocked and wanted to know more, but we didn't know how to talk about it.

The whole campus community would be informed by memo and everyone would know by Monday morning that Stan had been let go.

Dr. John Mecartney and Coach Glenn Snyder were two of the college professors who knocked on our door in the days that followed to give support and offer help to contest any injustice. There were also a couple of friends from the Berne church who wanted to help since they knew Stan from days working together on the Ft. Wayne church planting project.

Everyone who wanted to hear our side of the story got the same answer: "We don't know how to explain what happened. We came here to help Bluffton, not to cause problems." We thanked them for caring, but we let it go at that. We made no effort to defend ourselves. We did not want to discredit anyone. It seemed wiser to keep our mouths shut.

I called his boss's office and asked if I could see him. I needed to understand what had happened. His secretary checked with him and gave me an appointment. Several hours later, she called back to say that her boss was willing to see me but that I'd need to bring Stan along. I couldn't imagine asking Stan to go with me. He was bruised and punished enough. I felt it would be like a mother taking her child by the ear to go see his teacher for an explanation of his misbehavior.

I struggled, not knowing what to do. Finally, I sent a note telling him that I'd found insight in the prayer credited to both St. Francis and Reinhold Niebuhr: *"God grant me the serenity to accept the things I cannot change, the courage to change the things I can, and the wisdom to know the difference."* I cancelled the appointment although what I really wanted and truly needed was an explanation to help me understand what had gone wrong. It had not been my intent at all to change his decision.

The Wiebes, our best friends from Ft. Wayne days, had invited us to spend a few days of our Christmas vacation with them in New York City; Pastor Len was on sabbatical at Union Theological Seminary. We called them to cancel our plans, but they wouldn't hear of it. Joan said, "You need to get away for a few days more than ever now." They insisted that we come. Indeed, it was wonderful just to be with dear friends.

Among other interesting activities, they took us to see Greenwich Village, which was known at the time as New York's hippie and drug haven, with policemen walking the streets and guarding doorways in twos. We also saw the TV bar where everybody knows your name. It was a different world and a distraction from issues we faced at home.

The following poem is a reflection on that New Year's Eve together as the decade of the 1960's turned to 1970 --a new decade with the possibility of a better and more stable world both personally and universally.

New Year's Eve

The line waiting outside
David Letterman's Late Show theater
is strangely reminiscent
of an unemployment line.
New Yorkers and out-of-towners jockey
to find good times in an atmosphere that's warm
    --diversion from the shivering multitude
    of fears that ride the spine and rattle the brain.
    But a studio aid, garbed in red and black, gold braid
    at broad shoulders, opens the door to deliver
    some well-practiced sympathy, "Sorry.
Tickets are gone. You need to move on."
The crowd grumbles and heaves a chorus of sighs
clouding this already near-zero night.

I tug at my tan woolen scarf to relieve an itch,
"Might as well head over toward Times Square."
(Before leaving home we'd watched TV promo clips:
--A wounded Dick Clark cheerfully struggled
to enunciate a hard-won assurance
that the party is set to go on.)

I grasp my husband's arm,
shoulder bag tucked safely between us.
Folks heading our way on the salty sidewalk
step around a man, lying crumpled, passed
    out beside a brick wall, his bottle
    protruding from a paper sack at his side.
Two laughing teenagers stop
long enough to take a whiz on him,
and a voice from the crowd behind us opines,

"Isn't that just the way it is?"
My nose begins to weep and I fish for a tissue.

We duck into a coffee shop on the corner
unwittingly in time to watch three men assist
  a sickened companion who cannot walk
  but has been ordered to leave.
His shoe gets caught in the revolving door
  and is left behind on the snow-slopped floor.
The aroma of coffee beans is obliterated by alcohol;
so with no stomach left for java, we return to the street.
A sailor in navy and white dress uniform reels
  toward a surprised but beautiful girl—
  his arms open wide, offering embrace.

At Times Square a long center aisle cordoned off for cops
imprisons those paid to protect and aid
  the thousands crowded there
  seeking to celebrate.
Impatient commands: "Move it over, Buddy," and
impersonal greetings, "Hap-p-y New Year"
  are chattered through biting air.

The bright-lit crystal sphere hangs high above
  glaring billboards with much to sell--
  but beneath an empty-blackboard sky.
All of us know that Cinderella's glass slipper hour
  is fast approaching.
The crystal ball begins its slow descent
  while we wait and watch
in the slush below.

As brave as I wanted to be when it was time for us to return to the metaphorical slush in Bluffton, I was unsuccessful at hiding my tears.

It has taken me over fifty years to mull over the various bits and pieces of this painful story and come to some satisfactory and fuller understanding of the situation which altered our confidence and our lives. (See the epilogue at the end of this chapter.)

Stan knew that he needed to look right away for work. We really would like to have moved somewhere far away from Bluffton and just disappear from the community. But we had purchased a lot on which to build another home of our own, and two days before Stan was let go, space for the basement had been dug. We were stuck. Surely no one would purchase a lot that had a big hole in it. We had a signed contract with Maynard Badertscher and had no financial leeway other than to go ahead and build. Besides that, I had two more semesters of part-time schooling, including student teaching, before work for my Bachelor of Arts degree would be complete. We had to stay.

Opportunities for employment in Bluffton were few even in good economic times but to make matters worse, the country was experiencing another recession. Life looked very bleak. I'm certain that my prayers were full of questions. "Did we misunderstand what had seemed so clearly to be your guidance and provision? What do we do now? How are we to understand what has happened?"

Nevertheless, after being fired on Friday, Stan mustered up his courage on Monday morning and went down to Triplett Corporation (the only company of any size in Bluffton at that time) to apply for a job. The day was cloudy and gray. The children had gone to school. I sat on our couch, bible and devotional materials in hand, my heart filled with longing for Stan's success and for the welfare of our children. I prayed that Stan would be able to find a job, even though the recession and the small town made the possibility seem very remote.

He had been gone a little over an hour and a half when glorious sunshine broke through the clouds filling the living room with light and hope. I felt in my bones that he had found employment.

(Stan stayed with Triplett's Marketing and Advertising Department for the next sixteen years receiving appreciated raises and promotions. He was proud to represent their excellent products.)

I thought I simply couldn't go back to classes and face the other students, but that same Monday afternoon I had to go take my mid-term Ed Psych exam. Fighting emotion, I went. And I passed.

I was also taking an English Seminar in which I was doing a project of original poetry, and the following semester I took a course in creative writing. Poetry was an important way for me to process personal experience. I frequently reexamined my understanding of what had seemed to be God's provision for us when we made the move to Bluffton. The following poem speaks the tension between questioning and faith.

(UN)CERTAINTY

Stinging winds blow hot and wide
Across the wilderness of my heart.
Thoughts of Egypt: To return,
And temptation to rebel
Threaten sometimes
To reduce the pillar
Of cloud and fire.
Might it be a mere mirage
In the lonely desert?
But remembering the Red Sea path
        I wander on
and wonder.

Faith does not deny the heavy darkness of walking through streets of despair as I expressed it in this piece:

Hopeless Hope

Sunlight takes its way of fading
While daytime hours tick into dusk.
Charitable street lights flick on
Offering silly spots of advice--
Pathetic solutions to darkness.
Black night deepens; dawn delays.
Complicating clouds settle silently
And the transcendent lights maintain
Their grotesque glare --beaming out
Hypocrite haloes, brightly denying
The dreadful, dense, distance to dawn.

Much of the poetry written during this time was written through tears. Imagery from a storm the previous summer unfolded in a way that spoke of our family's experience. Like many of my poems, it contains a prayer.

The Storm

Standing here at the end of February
I remember the summer storm--
unexpected in the midst of a gentle rain.
I left the shirt, the ironing board
the memorizing of textbook facts
to check on the children.
The rain was coming faster now. . .
What I saw from my window
I understood --and loved.
Childhood was prancing in soggy green grass
dancing on tiptoe
flapping someday wings
against sopping blue denim.

Suddenly, the sky grew dark.
Leaves began to twist and turn
in helpless plea for shelter.
The rain, pounding now,
the wind siren,
struck terror in my soul.
Forcing open the door, I called to the children.
Like a mother hen protecting her chicks
I pulled them inside
As an ominous sheet of grey wind and rain rolled
into a wild whirlpool
and whipped our world
for hour-long seconds.

Amid the din and chaos
large limbs broke and crashed into the clearing
where moments before the children had played.
After the storm
we ventured outside
to survey destruction.
"A tree in front of Lovgren's," someone said,
"Out by the cemetery--
all over town in fact."
Then the news which pains me yet,
"The Beeshy maples:
One of them has fallen."
It couldn't be!

It happened at our backyard line
but in the storm-noise we had not heard it go.
Neighbors gathered near to view the sight;
They spoke with deep emotion and remembered
the neighborhood landmark
--centenarian twins, Black Maples.
Each tree, a bit one-sided on its own,
had balanced the other in nature's perfection
--a pattern of complements.
I recalled ecstatic joy I'd felt
first seeing the stately trees,
matched symmetry silhouetted,
transformed with autumn's Midas touch.

I knew then that someday I would write of them. . .
Now half my poem lay in splinters, prostrate on the ground
--the other half stood awkward and alone.
We examined the broken guardian of our hill

studied its weakness and still we wondered.
Why did it have to be?
One does not question the Ruler of the Universe;
he does, however, try to understand.
Was the tree's weakness that great --that central
Or did the fury of the storm hit in a peculiar way?
And what about the tree that's left?
Is it as strong as it appears to be
or is it vulnerable too?

The sky looks cold this winter's day
as I turn to the campus view;
the world is stripped of life.
My window scene has lost its charm
and it can never be the same
for innocence has passed me by.
I think about the summer storm--
about the empty spaces in the tree.
"God," I pray,
"Strengthen that which still remains--
Help repair each fault that might betray it.
I could not bear to see it cut up too
and cleared away."

Since the poem had been written for a class, I knew there was a possibility that it would be considered for publication in *The Centaur: an Interterm Journal of Opinion*. I was afraid everyone would know what it was about. And then I was afraid nobody would know. I hated it. I loved it. In the end, I risked it.

The real encouragement that it had been worthwhile for me to share it came one day after it had been published. A group of professors and students had been discussing the "power of the personal." One of the professors asked me if the Administrator of the Oaklawn mental health facility in Elkhart, had been in touch with me to say how much he appreciated the poem. He did not know me or my family, but he did know, in a much more serious situation, what it was like to live through a storm and about the need to forgive. Just a few years earlier, his wife had been murdered in their own home while he was at work and the children were at school. The person who committed the crime was never found, but many people thought it was probably someone who was mentally unbalanced and wanted to hurt the doctor and his family.

My creative writing professor wrote a lengthy response to that poem as well. He said, "If you tell your 'story' accurately and faithfully there will always be someone to hear the message as you intended it."

It is therapeutic to write out one's pain. It is also therapeutic to know that someone else has been helped by it.

One elective course I chose in the Spring of 1970 was Christian Faith taught by Dr. Paul Shelly, the professor whose efforts first brought me to Bluffton College back in 1952. We all knew that he was now dying with cancer, yet he continued to teach. I saw him uptown a couple of weeks after his right arm and lymph nodes had been amputated. I wanted to talk about how he was getting along, but he wanted to know about me.

"In the light of what has happened at the college," he said, "I have been wondering if you still feel that God led you back to Bluffton." Tears came immediately to my eyes as I answered him truthfully, "Dr. Shelly, if I don't have that, I don't have anything." He nodded his head, clearly relieved. "That's all I needed to know," he said. "That's all I needed to know." He knew first-hand that a Christian's life was not all roses.

Needing help with a variety of things now that he had just one arm, he had moved in with his sister and her family. I wanted to do something special that would buoy his spirit and remind him of the communion we have in Jesus Christ; so, instead of sending a bouquet or candy, I purchased two Teflon bread pans. Over the next couple of months, I made fresh loaves of whole wheat and honey bread to take to him and his sister's family. I'd make two loaves each time, one loaf for them and one for my own family. As I kneaded and shaped the dough, I prayed for his wellbeing and that he would feel himself surrounded with God's love. In spite of his pain and the struggle of learning to live with only one arm, he taught that last course in Christian Faith to the very end of the term and turned in his grades. A few days later, he died. For years, those Dr. Shelly bread pans kept turning out crusty loaves and warm prayers on behalf of people who for one reason or another were hurting.

It seems ironic that I could care so much for others; but still be experiencing the pain of feeling rejected –of never being good enough. The rejection and shame I felt when Dad left our family was underscored and heightened when my husband was rejected.

Years later, after studying spiritual formation and guidance I came to understand that "the dark night of the soul" is prime time for continued spiritual growth. We come to realize that even though our loved ones and we ourselves are not perfect, God accepts and loves us as we are. Psalm 30 speaks of being lifted out of sadness. It is still difficult for me to think that my best is good enough. It is depending upon God's grace and power that helps us to reach out to others --depending upon the Holy Spirit to flow through us and trusting the outcome to our God of Love and Compassion.

My last big challenge before graduation was student teaching. My cooperating teacher, Jean Roberts, was outstanding, and I had the opportunity to observe her teaching Shawnee High School's gifted students before I needed to take over her classroom.

Watching her on the Friday morning before I was to assume full responsibility for her classes the next week, I was overcome with a sense of my inadequacy.

My supervisor from Bluffton's Education Department, Professor Archie Perry, was supposed to meet with me after lunch at the school that day to see how things were going. I didn't want the students or my cooperating teacher to see them, but by the time that classroom session was over, tears were leaking down my cheeks. I just knew I could never succeed as a teacher. I was going to drop student teaching. The bell rang. I had to quickly find a phone so I could tell Professor Perry not to come.

I hurried out the door and there he was coming down the hall. He had arrived over an hour early. "I was just going to call you." I explained, "I can't do this. I'm going to drop student teaching. You didn't need to come."

The hallway was filled with students changing classes. Professor Perry took my arm and gently guided me to the teacher's lounge where he moved two chairs to face a window instead of the door where teachers were coming and going. As we sat down, he put his big black arm compassionately around me and encouraged me to tell him what was going on.

I don't remember exactly what he said those many years ago, but I do remember the essence. He told me that the reason I felt so insecure was that I was older and thus more aware of possible pitfalls than if I were younger and more filled with self-confidence. He tried to convince me that I didn't have to be perfect in order to be a good teacher. I wasn't convinced that I could meet the requirements and expectations of others, but I agreed to give it a try.

To make a long story short, after I'd finished my practice teaching, student evaluations as well as the report of my cooperating teacher indicated I'd done well.

I wish I could say that my heart was completely healed when

graduation time rolled around, but it obviously was not. Even though I'd achieved a goal of having a grade-point average high enough to be named to the PiDelta Society (3.7), I didn't feel like celebrating.

I didn't invite anyone to attend commencement ceremonies. Of course, Stan and our two children knew I was graduating and they would be there to support me. After the ceremonies, I discovered that my brother, Don, and his wife had come from Ft. Wayne. Since Don was a former BC student, they had received routine information from the college about commencement weekend. They wanted to be present for my "special day."

As I walked across the stage in Founders Hall to receive my diploma, I felt no joy in having achieved my dream of earning a college degree. When I got out in the hall, I had a strong urge to tear up the diploma. But I didn't do it.

The sharp lesson that day was that grieving a loss or trying to move beyond painful circumstances takes a while. Memories emerge at inconvenient or unexpected times. More healing was obviously needed in spite of my having granted forgiveness earlier.

Questions for Individual Reflection and or Group Sharing:

1. What do you think about a Christian being cynical about national or world affairs and about openly admitting depression?

2. Have you ever felt that it was or is God offering new opportunity and opening doors in response to need, desire, or prayer? If so, did you ever have reason to question whether you misunderstood?

3. Has God spoken directly to you through Scripture in response to a very current need?

4. Are there other questions that this chapter raises for you?

Epilogue to this chapter:

Stan's work as Director of Financial Aid included serving as a half-time Assistant in Development. I was far too busy to be as cognizant as perhaps I should have been of the national recession, the college's economic straits, and the heaviness of Stan's work-load.

The college had just built a much-needed maintenance building which, of course, was not an income producing investment. President Nixon and Congress were working on a bill regarding financial aid for students and it looked as though it was going to pass; therefore, Stan asked advice from the respected and newly retired comptroller about the advisability of extending student loans based upon the very likely passage of that bill. After that conversation, Stan felt encouraged to move ahead. He granted loans of approximately $60,000 to students who depended upon that financial aid in order to continue their schooling into the second semester. All were counting on Congress to pass the bill which was slated to provide for that assistance. But then the bill did not pass.

Student enrollment was also down. Stan was asked to drop his half-time responsibilities in the Development Department, stay on as Director of Financial Aid and become Director of Admissions as well. He was giving his all to those incredibly large assignments for which no one had been available to provide training.

One thing Stan was told at the time he was let go was that his staff had lost confidence in him. Obviously, the administration had as well. Poor Stan! He also wasn't bringing in as many new students as the college clearly needed.

It was ten or more years later that I learned what had been happening to all colleges and universities in those years. It wasn't just Bluffton that was having difficulty getting more students. At one of the President's Club dinners for donors, President Neufeld showed a graph indicating the national drop in college enrollment during the late 1960's and early 1970's. I then realized it hadn't been all Stan's fault that Bluffton's enrollment was down. Clearly, he had been struggling in an impossible and very complex position. I certainly wish that I had been able to understand back then what all colleges had been experiencing during those difficult days.

Years later, after studying spiritual formation and guidance, I recognized and began to understand the "dark night of the soul" that I experienced back then. The "dark night" is prime time for continued spiritual growth. It is in trusting that our ever-present God is with us as we walk through life's dark valleys whether it feels like it or not.

Believing in God's presence, guidance, and grace gives me courage to reach out and try to serve others even though I feel inadequate.

Stan's later success at Triplett Corporation and still later as a financial advisor with Ameriprise has helped me realize that he was best suited for employment where he did not have to supervise others. He was truly a good, hard-working, and trustworthy man. I could not have asked for a more supportive husband as I accepted responsibilities and challenges that were ahead for me.

chapter 9

Employing Faith and Love in the Classroom

I now had a degree in Comprehensive English, and I needed to find employment to repay the tuition debt I'd incurred for my last semester because our status at the college had changed. I believed that my past work experience and my scholastic record would assure me of a job. I sent applications to several schools in the vicinity, but there was a backlog of teachers and the only way to even be considered was to get one's foot in the door by serving as a substitute until a full-time position opened up. I was disappointed.

September came and went. I reluctantly accepted the few calls where a substitute was needed, but I didn't enjoy teaching without permanent student/teacher relationships. I remembered my former boss's encouragement to write. Maybe I was to be a writer after all. That sounded interesting, but very unsubstantial financially. I did a lot of praying, trying to understand my situation. The long-time assistant in the placement office at the college kept saying that there could well be some openings during the year. "There often are," she said.

There were days when I was downright depressed that I didn't have a regular job. I began to realize how hopeless people feel when they've been unemployed for a long time and really want to work.

I was willing to write if that was what I should do, but it was hard to get started. Finally, in November I made a sort of pact with myself and God that if I didn't have a permanent position by the end of the month, I'd figure I was supposed to write and I'd get serious about it. I got busy catching up with things that needed to be done in the house before I knew whether I was to be a teacher or a writer.

On the day my "pact" was running out, I got a call from the principal of Perry Middle School about half-an-hour away saying that her junior high English teacher's husband was being moved to another state. Would I consider taking her place?

I did. I learned a lot. The teacher in the room next to mine had little control over her classroom. It was clear that students did not respect her and everything seemed to be constantly in chaos. A big ex-Marine down the hall kept firm control of his students by using corporal punishment. I didn't want to be like either of them.

During that time, I was asked to teach the high-school age Sunday school class at church. I was hesitant to take on extra work when I was so new to my full-time job but soon discovered that the faith-focused aspect of that assignment actually gave me energy for my paying job in the public school. Go figure!

The next year, I was offered a job closer to home. Bluffton High School was only five minutes away and I liked the idea of being in the same system as my own children so that all my snow days, holidays, and vacations coincided with theirs.

I enjoyed working with teenagers. My notebooks of poetry written during those years reflect the spirit which I brought to my classroom. One poem was titled:

a teacher's prayer

thirty young people
i'm leading today

oh god, help me

show me the way
through facts

and through frictions
help us to grow

then above all
help them to know

i care

Many days, perhaps most, went well. But not all, of course. When conversations in the teachers' lounge turned negative, I could understand. I knew what sorts of classroom issues all teachers face. But I found joy in teaching students rather than merely teaching a subject. I received energy just walking into my classroom and realizing the potential that was waiting there for me. Perhaps this poem speaks about the reality of a difficult day:

Trying

Names penciled on Formica,
Soft gray against a hard white world,
Are easily erased, forgotten,
So is today at Bluffton High!

Great thoughts floated
Through fluorescent sunlight,
Most unnoticed and uncaught.
In the hub-bub some have learned
While others left untaught.

The radiator hiss
And the knocking broom
Outside my door
Remind me to bid the day goodbye
And let tomorrow come again
Clean and warm.

Alone in my classroom after everyone else had gone home, I often prayed for God's presence to so fill that space that it might be sensed there the following day. Sometimes I sat at my desk or on my stool at the lectern or even in a particular student's desk if he or she was having a problem of one sort or another.

I recall one bright young lady in particular who always got uptight at test time. She spoke to me about it. We both knew that if she could just relax, she could do better work. Knowing that she came from a Christian home, I suggested that she try prayer as a means of accessing a quieter mind and "letting go" of her tension.

One high school student committed suicide, and the daughter of a highly respected member of the community wrote in her journal that she often thought of suicide. Another journaled about considering an abortion and then asked if she could talk with me about it. I agreed, but just before our private appointment for that talk she ended the pregnancy. These students and others like them gained a special place in my heart and prayers because of the struggles I knew they were experiencing.

During my tenure as a teacher there were at least seven accidental student deaths. I had a book on my desk titled *The*

Geranium on the Windowsill Just Died, but Teacher, You Went Right On. I vowed that with each tragedy, we'd alter the next day's lesson plan and take time to journal memories of the student or thoughts about what had just happened. Some special poems resulted in those written reflections. Here's one of mine:

Time's Twisted Frame

Gray clouds race
The midnight skyway
To be separated in a lightning flash,
A thundering crash!
White metal incinerates
And gasoline paves
A purifying path
In the crackling silence.

Three Bluffton sons
Called townspeople together
Overcrowding our spacious funeral home.
Classmates, friends, and strangers
Stood by burdened caskets and
Shared cleansing tears.
Love, we learned,
Has far-reaching dimensions!

I considered my classroom to be as much a place of ministry as any church –not for preaching, but for caring in the Spirit of Jesus Christ.

Many years later, I was teaching a writing class for Bluffton University's Institute for Learning in Retirement when the assignment was to write about "telling the truth." Since I always did the assignments along with the members of the class, I chose to truthfully record an earlier incident in my high school classroom. Here's that story:

The Day One of My Students Told the Truth . . . And Got Away with It.

As a teacher, I knew about the "good student discounts" that automobile insurance companies offer to teenage drivers who earn and maintain a certain grade point average.

I was also aware that one of my student's classroom attitude had changed. He was a below average student in my English class, but a few weeks before grade-time, he had begun doing some of his homework and participating in discussions. It was a pleasant change.

What I did *not* know was that Walt's (the name has been changed) new behavior was motivated by the fact that his sixteenth birthday was coming up and he would soon be applying for his first driver's license. A poem that I wrote after school one day about my relationship with this student was therapy for me. Although it is addressed to him, I did *not* give him a copy. I share it here for a brief background synopsis of what happened. Then I'll tell "the rest of the story." It also reveals something about the way I tried to teach.

Back to the Basics

I decided to like you
on Day One
when you tried to antagonize
the teacher in me.
"Do we *have* to take this here course?
How soon can we drop it?"

You flashed a crooked smile --a smirk.
"We don't need no more English!
This here's a waste of time."

I smiled.
"I can see my work's cut out for me.
I accept the challenge to help you
enjoy the year."

I ignored
your smart-mouthed comments
and turned shallow answers
to profundities--
helping you to look good
among your peers.

We got along
amazingly well until
your insurance bill
came due at grade time.

What you had earned
caused you to spurn
me, who'd worked so hard
to plus your "C."

You tried to discount
my integrity
because your "company"
couldn't discount
the premium fee for
an "average" student driver.

Someone was at fault
and you chose to think
that it was I. The risk to me
increased.
You placed the blame
and spouted hatred
publicly.

We discussed the issue
privately.
I <u>had</u> decided to like you,
but it was getting harder
and seemingly less wise.

I decided then I'd have to
love you
although (or was it because?)
you seem so unlovable.

Certainly, you don't love
yourself.
I wondered if there could be
anyone who loved you--
so filled with resentment,
so tactless of tongue.

Day after day
I smiled and looked for ways
to help you build
honest confidence.

Today you lashed out again
at cherished values, scoffing
at things the class holds dear.

Once more I try to see the world
through your eyes
--to understand
rather than put you down.

I really don't want to
make you seem small
as you feel
or as unreasonable
as you are.

I know now
that I do not like you
and probably never shall.

But in spite of your ugliness
inside,
I know you still long to be
and need to "feel"
loved.

Loving is not listed
in the curriculum guide
for English Eleven,
and "feeling" loved

is not mentioned as a basic
minimum requirement.
However,

(Did you catch the transition?)
if I am to teach
and you are to learn
we're going to have to succeed
with the basics.

After he failed at getting me to change his "C+" to a "B," so he could get the good student discount on his insurance, I assured him that if he continued working as he had in the few weeks prior to grade-time, I felt sure he could earn the "B" he needed. Instead of trying, he chose to sulk. He now volunteered nothing in class discussions but a cold, disinterested stare. I couldn't tell whether his brain was engaged or not.

A few days later, after explaining the metric units of poetry and showing the class how those different units were put together in varying line lengths, I gave them a homework handout to help them work with the formal rhythm of words.

The next morning, the class and I were having great fun as students proved their understanding by sharing clever, original lines they had written to fit the assigned metrical rhythms. Walt was sitting sullenly in his seat, but his book was open. Suddenly, when I asked for the line of iambic dimeter, he quickly put up his hand, clearly eager to answer.

Perhaps I should explain here (or refresh your memory) that the iamb consists of one un accented and then one accented syllable. And the dimeter calls for two units of the iamb put together. That rhythm on paper would look like "./ ./" and would sound like, "da **DUM**, da **DUM**."

Pleased that my difficult student was volunteering after several days of hostile silence, I called on him. His response was louder than usual. And it was correct. With obvious pleasure and in a spirit that could not be denied, he said, "I **HATE** your **GUTS!**"

There was a corporate gasp in the classroom. The unthinkable had been said with certainty, and he smirked with a delighted sense of having pulled a fast one on the teacher. The class looked as though they had been slapped. They were offended by what had been said. We all knew he meant it.

I was shocked! I'm sure there must have been a bit of a pause while we all absorbed what had just happened --and Walt must have enjoyed his moment of risky triumph. Perhaps it seemed to him that it would be worth whatever the result might be.

I didn't miss a beat though. I could never have planned ahead for this situation, but the confident response was right there on my lips. I didn't have to think twice. You're **right,"** I said. You're absolutely right --da **DUM**, da **DUM**." And then reflectively I repeated his words as though there was nothing personal in them at all: "I hate your guts. --That's iambic dimeter. Does anybody else have an example they'd like to share?" And the class went right on.

> ***A gentle answer turns away wrath, but a harsh word stirs up anger. The tongue of the wise adorns knowledge. . .***
>
> **--Proverbs 15:1-2a NIV**

I won't deny that the atmosphere was sort of filled with ozone --like after lightning strikes. Something was different. I'm guessing that everyone was wondering why I hadn't verbally "put him in his place" or sent him to the principal's office. Instead, I accepted his anger and graced him with credit where credit was due.

As I write now about this event that happened many years ago, I think of the way that student got away with telling the truth that day. I also think of students we read about these days who obviously feel unloved and who are so bottled up with anger that they let guns speak for them.

No, I don't approve of students or anyone else bad-mouthing others, but somehow that day I knew that I needed to let the truth stand. He needed that chance to vent. I hoped the class would defend me in their own minds and hearts. I credited him with what was right about what he said rather than reprimanding him over what was wrong. I felt he needed to be understood and loved more than he needed to be punished.

The following poem was written one Advent season while my classes were reading Shakespeare's *Macbeth,* and Bluffton University's Drama Department was presenting Thornton Wilder's *Our Town.*

Impromptu Reward

Christmas spots the light
straight above our stable stage,
wiping out the shadows,
enabling us to play
our tiny love scenes,
straw and all,
without worry about audience
or applause--
without worry about lines.
The play is being written
day by day
and the practice
is the performance.

Each tender word or touch
is video-taped, recorded
in the heaven of our hearts,
and a star hung in that sky
beats a thousand lights
on the world's marquees.

Love, compassion and acts of caring in our everyday world are the things that really count. Our faith is expressed each day in the way we live.

The next two poems speak of professors whose words and actions expressed God's caring for me. Each of them made a significant difference when I needed courage beyond my own.

In the previous chapter, I wrote about having to take a mid-term exam when my hurting mind and heart were filled with emotion. It was years later when I was teaching at the high school that Dr. Schellenberg, my Ed Psych professor, died. The Basinger Funeral Home was directly across the street from my second-story classroom windows.

Memories of him will always be linked with my most difficult test day –the Monday after Stan was let go.

To My Ed Psych Professor

The life of this one day is over now
and I stand alone in my own classroom
remembering yours.
Examination time had come
just as my world was newly shattered.
I'd wanted to skip class forever.
Wisely, you knew I was swallowing pride
as I joined the room of younger students,
all of us needing to pass the test at hand.

Warmly, you reached out to me
in common conversation
accepting the counterfeit bravery
of a painted smile quivering
above clouds hanging low in my heart.
You ignored threatening rain in my eyes
but in my pain you left me not alone.

Compassion tempered every word;
your words came far too fast
for me not to know you knew, but
I loved you for not touching the wound.
Afterward, I left alone, knowing
that you were with me all the way.

Today, you lie across College Avenue
in the funeral home alone. Standing at
my classroom window, lifting the shades
of my mind, I am with you even though
visiting hours have not yet begun.
I am seeing your life, not your coffin.

Time rolls relentlessly on,
yet eternity lies in moments of caring.
Despite life-dealt disasters
neither of us has died
nor are we alone.

That musing inspired yet another poem about Dr. Schellenberg and the important part both he and Professor Archie Perry, my student teaching supervisor, had played in my life. Both men were God given gifts when I needed support "with skin on." They cared for me and deepened my ability to care later for my own students. I am grateful to them and to God.

The Oak (*Quercus alba)* represents Dr. Schellenberg and the Ebony *(Diospyros ebenum)* represents Professor Archie Perry because he was African American.

To *Quercus alba* and *Diospyros ebenum*

The woods is full of trees
but to each child
there is one or ones
especially strong
and tall.

Compassionate boughs bend:
to hold the seeking one,
shading him
in the withering watch
of the day

renewing him for return
to a world
of common day people
and places.

Trees and children
whisper to one another
in gentle touch
and tone

But others do not feel
or comprehend--
though many
stand nearby.

In a mystical moment
one life finds courage to be
while the other is affirmed
in its purpose
for being.

The final poem in this chapter speaks of both inspiring and destructive ways of teaching. I had eagerly anticipated my first graduate school course at Bowling Green State University. It was a summer course in creative writing that focused on poetry. The professor in the second stanza, whose name has been blocked from my memory, had to be the worst I ever encountered. I aspired to be like the teacher in the first stanza.

Two Teachers

One was like a lighted match
Touching unused wicks
--Waiting
For the flame to catch
And burn.

The second was brass domed,
A long-handled critic
Snuffing out light
Even under the halo
Of self-respect.

At the time I didn't recognize the positive lesson I was learning from a very negative experience but the poem that emerged helped me to see what kind of teacher I definitely did not want to be. Even awful experiences can be used for good in God's kingdom.

Questions for Individual Reflection and or Group Sharing

1. Have you ever been in a contentious situation where you intentionally responded with a gentle or loving answer instead of with harsh words that would have stirred up more anger? How did it work?

2. What teachers or professors made a real difference in your life? Share those stories.

3. What were the difficult and/or particularly good times at your place of employment that have made a difference in the person you have become?

4. Do you have particular stories about opportunities that seem to have come from God to help you help others?

chapter 10

Mid-Life Crisis and Questioning

I do not know exactly when the feelings of restlessness began. Kim was married and Jeff had graduated from high school. I remember periodically questioning whether or not I should stay in teaching. Grading so many papers seemed like such a thankless job. I wondered if my responses to things they wrote were appreciated, or if my red-penciled corrections to their punctuation and grammar changed their understanding. I was dreading the thought of another school year.

Then one day in late August the mail carrier delivered inspiration that renewed my spirit and broadened my outlook beyond discouragement. The timing felt like God's answer to my felt need for life-giving purpose. It came in an editorial on the back page of *The Mennonite,* our denominational magazine. The editor had chosen a back-to-school theme.

"Teachers," he wrote, "are in a unique position to influence the lives of the young. Whether Christian teachers are in public schools or private, they are performing Christian service as they reach beyond the curriculum to care and love."

Tears rolled down my cheeks as I read. I knew, of course, that teaching is a sacred calling.

I returned to the classroom that September filled with

renewed enthusiasm. My ideal philosophy of teaching had been affirmed. Although I had never experienced a special sense of call to be a teacher, the profession had fit well with having school-age children. I felt I was where God could use me.

In the Spring, however, restlessness returned. I had served on a State committee and then was invited to help write standardized tests to be used throughout the State –a request that made me uncomfortable. I didn't like the idea of teachers having to "teach for testing" instead of teaching more creatively in relationship with students.

Administrator evaluations were always flattering; they made me feel more successful on the outside than I felt on the inside. I struggled with my feeling of just never being good enough. My spirit felt singed. "*Is this what burn-out feels like*?" I asked myself. "*If that's my problem, perhaps I need a year-long leave of absence.*"

"Lord," I prayed, "please give me a sense of direction, a renewed sense of meaning and purpose."

Students and colleagues as well as members of my prayer group were unaware of my serious questionings; however, family members were aware of the stress. One week-end in particular, I realized that my life had gotten out of control. One journal entry deals with my frustration:

> *I want to say, "Lord, go with me." But perhaps I should say, "Lord, I'll go with you." Would God take me to work and to the commitments that I have made? Right now, I don't know what else to do. "Let me praise you, Lord, with my life and let my life be a blessing to others. I am trying to listen, Lord. Really, I am."*

But how could I possibly give up teaching? I had received my Master's Degree and was near the top of the salary scale. I had tenure. The School Board was paying every dime of my family's Blue Cross Plan with Major Medical Coverage; they even provided dental insurance. The State Teachers' Retirement Program was one of the best if I'd just stay with it. I had summers off.

My husband couldn't imagine why I'd consider giving up a career like that.

During these months of discernment, I was fine at school. I had a job to do and I did it. But on week-ends. . .

One day, when I was feeling emotionally strong and thought I could discuss my situation rationally, I called my pastor, Mel Schmidt, for an appointment.

"I want to discuss a mid-life crisis," I said. "And no, Stan and I are not having marital difficulties." I laughed, feeling rather clever that I could make a joke about my turmoil. Despite the fact that Pastor Schmidt was extremely busy with Holy Week plans and programs, he said he'd see me the next morning.

By the time I got to his office, my emotions had sabotaged my resolve to discuss the matter objectively. With an ugly red nose and tear-stained cheeks, I stepped into his office. "I hope you've got a couple of good jokes," I said, "because I sure need them."

He didn't have any jokes to tell, but he was a good listener. And I was eager to hear what he'd have to say. I realized that he could tell me, as the editorial had previously, that teaching was an important service. I was truly willing to hear that if it was what God wanted said to me. I realized that I could leave that office with a whole new dedication to teaching. And that would be great! I just needed new motivation.

He said none of those comfortable, traditional things that I would have recognized as true about my profession. Instead, he spoke of faith that enables people to take risks. That also rang true. Jesus left security behind when he chose to walk God's way for him.

As I was leaving, Pastor Schmidt said, "If Easter means anything, Ruth, it means leaving what feels dead behind you and walking out in newness of life. That is the resurrection." His words were following the same path as my devotions and my heart. But how would I convince my mind to do such an irrational thing?

Alive Now inadvertently offered another page of advice. White space surrounded and set apart a single quotation which artistically and spiritually compelled me:

> **Proceed with much prayer, and your way will be made plain.**
>
> **--John Wesley to Ellen Gretton, 1782.**

I copied that quotation in my heart, and it carries a continuing truth for me. To this day, I share it with others who are seeking God's leading in their lives.

I toyed with the idea of just asking for a leave of absence. A leave seemed like a sensible option which would protect my job and myself while checking out what it would be like not to teach. But God seemed to say to me, "Ruth, do you trust me or don't you?"

A poem in *Alive Now* challenged me:

YOU CAN

You can stay in Egypt and
settle for surrender of
self and freedom. . .
here there is
a womblike
protection. . .
but the view is limited

OR
you can exodus
into the beckoning
of a new future, a
new human hope. . .
and then go back
to Egypt where
Pharaoh will take care of you

OR
you can exodus
into the unknown
wilderness and
discover a
Promised Land
of identity,
maturity, and
perpetual struggle
filled with pain
and joy, agony
and ecstasy,
dying and coming
alive again,
challenge and
change.

--William McElhanney, *Celebrations on Coming Alive*
(used with permission)

For years I'd been serving on committees and boards of our local, district, and national levels of the General Conference Mennonite Church. This particular year, I was helping as a playful daily news reporter for the Central District meetings at Oak Grove Church and had a great time summing up in an entertaining manner what was happening daily. One of the announcements I was asked to read to the delegates was about the need for an editor at the General Conference headquarters located in Newton, Kansas. It sounded half interesting. I wondered. . . . The children were gone and on their own, but it would mean a major move for Stan and me.

In late spring I received an invitation from Ohio Northern University to attend an appreciation "dessert and program" for cooperating teachers and the university students who had been observing in their public-school classrooms. A noted author and educator would be speaking. I really didn't want to go. I was busy --as usual. But more than that, I was becoming more and more certain that I wanted to resign when the school year was over. Why would I want to hear a presentation now that would undoubtedly promote enthusiasm for teaching? Hadn't I been confused enough already?

But I thought of the young man who had been observing in my classroom and I didn't want to let him down by not attending with him.

I was in for a surprise! In my journal I recorded what this speaker had to say to his audience of teachers and future teachers:

> *He said that if you are truly an educated person, rather than just 'trained to be a teacher,' you probably will not remain a teacher all your life. You'll be equipped for more than just teaching.*

What a strange thing for someone to say in that setting! His words were not wasted on me. (Many years later, it occurred to me that he might have been referring to the real possibility that some would move into school administration, but that did not occur to me that evening. I heard it as God's voice pointing me to a career change.)

Stan and I attended the Bluffton College baccalaureate service in May. One of the speakers was a woman about my age. Like me, she had quit work at one point to be a full-time wife and mother. Then she went back to school and became a registered nurse. Now she was graduating with a B.A. degree. People often ask her, she said, how she knows when she's reached a new turning point in her life. She gave us her answer:

> *"God has created intuitive instincts in his creatures. Just as geese know when the seasons change, we too can know," she said. "No one has to tell geese when to fly south. They just know."*

I felt Stan turn to look at me. Tears glistened in his eyes, and he smiled as he noted mine. I knew then that his heart was beginning to understand. As I pointed out to him later, "It's important to know when you are a goose."

The week after school was out, I resigned. I had been a teacher for thirteen years.

Questions for Individual Reflection and or Group Sharing

1. Has a sense of God's leading affected your career choices and/or changes?

2. Has a feeling of restlessness ever challenged you to consider making a change of some sort?

3. What specific experiences have you had that either affirmed or caused you to question your current involvement (large or small) or your direction in life?

chapter 11

Career Change

So what do I do now? I have resigned from a really good career and I have no idea what I'm going to do next. A poem written during that time of unknowing shows what I was feeling.

Facing a Mid-Life Change

Now I know
how Noah felt
when God told him
to build an ark
and nobody else
knew it was going to rain.

It seems so strange
to prepare for change,
close books on life thus far,
to sort things out
and wait for things
to rearrange.

The rains are coming;
the feeling
floods my brain.
They may be showers that
merely bring new growth;
they could be storms
that wash away past gain.

Help me to learn
from Noah's faith
that my world
can be renewed.
Help me select
the needful things
as I walk on with you.

I believe that God often gives us just enough light for one step at a time. And when we take that step, there is light enough for the next step. "Okay, God, I've taken a mighty big step. So what's next?"

Two weeks before the school year ended, I had told my small bible study/prayer group in confidence that I was thinking seriously about leaving my position at the school. I admitted that it seemed like a crazy move but I was feeling led toward change.

Mark Weidner, our Central District Conference Minister as well as a member of First Mennonite Church, spoke up with authority in his tone, "Ruth, you ought to apply for the position of Associate Pastor at Church."

I scoffed. Never had I considered such a thing! Me? A contemplative Quaker at heart be a *paid-staff* minister?

I had chaired the Pastoral Search Committee that brought Melvin Schmidt from Wichita to Bluffton, and I knew that the church would soon want to hire an assistant or associate, but ME?

No way. Absolutely no way. That thought had never entered my mind. I couldn't even imagine it.

I wrote to our denominational headquarters in Kansas and inquired about the general editor position that was being advertised. I knew our national church leaders as a result of having served six years on the Program Committee for our national assemblies. They knew me too from published articles and poems in denominational magazines. They replied that they also had an opening for General Secretary of Adult Education that might interest me, and they offered to fly me out to interview for both positions in Kansas.

There was no way I would accept a job in the Newton headquarters unless Stan was whole-heartedly in favor of changing jobs and finding work in the Newton or Wichita areas. I did not want him to give up the job security he'd earned unless he, too, was feeling a nudge to change. The fact that Penril had bought-out Triplett and that management employees were being phased-out caused Stan to suspect that the day would come when he too would be without a job there.

Our Sunday school class had already planned a retreat weekend at Camp Friedenswald in Michigan for soon after classes were finished at the college and public schools. Stan and I always participated in that sort of thing and we signed up to go. The retreat was over after lunch on Sunday, but Stan and I decided to take time to relax on the pier before heading home. Lying in the sunshine, we went to sleep. When we awakened, the first thing Stan said was, "Bunnie, if you think God might be calling you to Newton, I want you to go and check it out." (What a guy!) So I made arrangements to go.

I discovered that word about my resignation was getting around fast because I soon received a call from the former guidance counselor at Bluffton who was currently a principal at Allen East.

He wanted me to apply for an upper level English teaching job there. I didn't even consider the job at Allen East. If I wanted to teach, I'd surely stay where I was in Bluffton.

Dr. Elmer Neufeld, president at Bluffton College, called and wanted me to consider coming to work there. He said he didn't know just yet what the job might be, but he wanted to talk about possibilities. It wasn't long until I was asked to consider a position as Director of Church Relations for the college. When I turned that down, they came up with another newly created position for me to consider in the development area. At this point, the idea of working for the college held little or no appeal.

Stan started watching the Wichita paper for job openings. While I was interviewing in Newton, our church's congregational chairman, Bruce Shelly, called wanting to talk with me. When Stan said I was in Newton, he asked Stan to have me call him when I got home.

Stan dutifully gave me that message when I returned, but I was pretty sure about what Bruce wanted, and I really didn't want to consider the job at the church. I didn't return his call.

I found myself leaning toward the Education Department work in Newton because it offered more variety than editing, but I felt no clear leading. They told me that they could wait for as much as three months for my answer if I needed that long to decide and make arrangements.

About a week later, our congregational chairman called again and playfully began, "I heard you were visiting the Holy City." It was a delightfully humorous beginning to his request that we have lunch together and discuss the job at church. He informed me that he and some other members who had teenagers in the youth group thought I'd be perfect as youth leader and that being responsible for Christian education seemed to fit my gifts. Those were the parts of the Associate Pastor position that I had to admit seemed to be in line with what those who knew me locally perceived to be my strengths.

Stan was having no luck finding job openings that he could even apply for in Kansas. One day after he got home from work and we were relaxing on the porch he announced, "I'm thinking that I'd like to stay at Triplett for at least a year or two yet." As far as I was concerned, that sealed the deal about moving to Kansas.

I wanted to commit my future fully to God and my interest in things spiritual. I was just beginning to wonder if the church *might* be the place to which God was leading me –surprising and scary as it was. I would have to be interviewed by the deacons; their recommendation would have to be approved by Church Council, and then, since it was to be a full-time position, it meant that my name would have to be put before the congregation for a vote. This was the first time our whole congregation would be asked to approve a woman as one of their pastors. There had been a couple of part-time women on staff before, but they were simply appointed.

The whole issue of women in leadership and ministry was causing a hullabaloo in the whole Mennonite denomination as well as in many other denominations. If people voted against hiring me, would it be because I was a woman, or because they knew me and thought I wasn't an appropriate choice?

Quakerism teaches that all people, men and women alike, are called to be ministers, so I had no problem with the fact that my current church was ready to help change the religious culture.

I kept remembering a large but very simple walnut wall-hanging in the parlor of the girls' dorm at boarding school. In captivating gold letters was the following challenge:

Not to be ministered unto, but to minister.

--Matthew 20:28, KJV

That motto led to another poem:

But to Minister?
(Reflection on Mark 10:45 KJV)

"Not to be
ministered unto
but to minister."

A long wooden motto
lettered in gold
ministered in the parlor
to a young girl who
was afraid to minister
but did want to serve.

Might there be a way
or time to understand
and grow beyond
her cautious mind and
the wooden sign?

That remembered sign
lettered in gold
was taking its hold
on a life that would
reflect and consider
the message until

it re-membered
her heart.

I knew that the word "minister" was not limited to providing leadership in religious settings. Most newer translations of that verse use the word "serve" instead of "minister." I had always considered my work as a teacher to be a form of ministry. Indeed, I believe that we are all to be servants in God's kingdom. We are to be carriers of God's love. We can each be a part of God's presence and provision here on earth.

But if I had known that I would be called to what is often known as "public ministry in a church," I wonder if I would ever have had the courage or chutzpah to resign from teaching. I suppose I might have responded more easily if God had hit me over the head with his textbook and an even more direct passage, but I found myself responding to God as did Moses (recorded in Exodus 4:13 RSV) when he could not imagine himself in the role he was being called to fill: ***"Oh, my Lord, send, I pray, some other person."***

In the past, my finding what I believed to be God's guidance resulted from an interior sense of searching and eventually having a pretty good idea of what I should do or where I should go. But this was a matter of a call coming first from the outside. It was an uncomfortable challenge for me to put my future into the hands and opinions of others while I sought clarity.

A Prayer

I open my hands, Lord,
freeing the past
to fly away.

I open my hands
to the future
to take what comes
uncensored by fear

Knowing that your
Spirit can fill
each new gift

with purpose
knowing that your
Kingdom comes
to open hearts

and hands
and fills them to
overflowing.

Fill my hands
with your loving touch
to share.

I finally decided to go through the necessary local and district interviews. Then came the congregational vote. It was 89% in favor of calling me.

I'm sure I didn't fully understand what it would be like to preach at least once a month to our congregation of scholarly professors and intellectual professionals.

I clearly remember my first Sunday as part of the pastoral team. I was to be the worship leader and Pastor Schmidt was preaching. As we started together toward the front of the church at the beginning of the service, my knees felt like they were full of water and very unstable. Just as we went under the arch above the aisle, God's voice steadied me. "But I will be with you." That voice in my head was clear; my knees straightened up and I walked on with new courage.

Two years later at the time of my ordination, I remembered God's words to Moses as recorded in Exodus 3:5 RSV: ***". . .put***

off your shoes from your feet, for the place on which you are standing is holy ground." As I knelt for the blessing, I took off my shoes. I felt I was on holy ground.

My journal tells of insecurities, vulnerabilities, disappointments, and joys during the next twelve years. A few poems tell stories of those experiences as well.

A high school gymnast and former student of mine, though not a Mennonite, frequently stopped at my church office for conversation and a hug. She was fighting a constant battle with long-standing eating disorders and was receiving professional care for anorexia and bulimia. One day she came in tears and asked, "Mrs. Naylor, could you write a poem just for me? One that would give me hope to hang onto?

Though the ensuing poem was written specifically for her, it also speaks to me and for others who feel (or have felt) life's vulnerabilities.

The Circus Performer's Prayer

One step at a time, Lord,
one day at a time.
Sometimes it's all I can do
    to just hang on, and
some days again I can climb
toward that tight wire
of performance
where I need to stand alone--
    (Or am I ever really alone?)
and walk from one point
of security to another.

Keep me balanced, Lord!
I commit my will --and

all the gymnastic training
of my mind and body
to success. . .

Still, if I should be blinded
by the bright lights,
thrown off balance
by premature applause
or frightened by the darkness
o u t t h e r e
and below me,
remind me of the net
which Love spreads
under the thin wire I walk
to catch and bounce me back
giving me footing
to a ladder hold again--
not defeated, but stronger
each time than before
ready to climb again,
one small step at a time
day by day.

Help me not to focus on the wire,
the crowd, my weakness,
or my fears.
Help me, instead, to concentrate
on the goal
and to remember
Your invisible hand
in the universe
around and above me,
beckoning me to progress

--waiting patiently
when I'm too weary to move.

And then, Lord, assure me
that someday I will teach others
how to negotiate the tight thin wire
which has become my challenge.

My young friend carried the poem with her for a long time. I wish I could tell you that she recovered, but her heart eventually gave out. I was pleased that her family invited me to help with her memorial service at their church in town. It helped me deal with the heartbreak that goes with caring.

The following poem was written later, but it reflects feelings that so often surround us when we face what seem to be untimely deaths.

Cloudy Morning Prayer

Lord, walk with us
on this strange road
to Emmaus. It is so
hard to recognize purpose
and hope in the midst
of broken dreams
and death.

Our hearts,
torn and confused,
cry out to you,
"Lord, walk with us in this
place where earth's dust
swirls up to cloud our eyes
and threatens to choke us."

I'd never noticed before that giving always fell short of the church's spending plan. Now I know that it's almost always that way, but back then I felt it was because the congregation could not or did not want to afford two full-time pastors. I also knew that I was not equipped to handle everything that needed to be done. Admittedly, my desire to be better than my best was one of my problems. I was not at all good at turning a blind eye to others' wishes and/or expectations --nor was I good at self-care. I was aware that my monthly sermons did not contain the scholarly exposition that the highly educated members of the congregation would have appreciated. I was a bit too much of a mystic, I think –one who depended more upon sharing the contemporary experience of faith. One professor told me that my prayers were too poetic.

After a few years I asked to be cut back to ¾ time so the church could hire a half-time Director of Christian Education with creative ideas and better ability to recruit teachers for the children's classes.

The congregation encouraged and facilitated my desire for more seminary education. I had already taken a few courses, including Anabaptist History, at Associated Mennonite Biblical Seminary in Elkhart, IN, and Clinical Pastoral Education at Lutheran Hospital in Ft. Wayne. I truly enjoyed one-on-one pastoral care, and it felt good to officiate at many funerals and some of the weddings.

A few more years passed before I was out of energy and fresh ideas for the Youth Program. In addition to meeting regularly, we had attended denominational youth conventions, done a number of service and learning trips, and attended winter retreats at camp –all of which required fund raising for those special events.

Murky Reflection

Soul thirsty, I walk
to the water's edge
but a mid-day storm
has muddied the gift
I came to receive.

I sit silently awhile,
watching the current
dodge rocks in its way.
At last, I lie back
with a stone for a pillow.

Then dreaming,
the water seems to clear
and my ears awaken.
The stream is singing
"This life flows on. . ."

Startled and alert now,
I meditate on the hope
that called me to this place,
and grant the river her right
to be unclear at times.

I really wanted to quit working altogether. I handed in my resignation so the church could hire some fresh blood, but the powers-that-be came back with a plan that would have me stay on half-time as Senior Visitation Pastor. I agreed to continue serving in that capacity.

I have a history of internal questions resulting from different Quaker and Mennonite beliefs about rituals in the church –particularly baptism.

It began when I was denied full membership at the Maplewood Mennonite Church which Stan and I helped to start while living in Ft. Wayne. The time had come to create an official list of Charter Members. All who belonged to other churches were required to present a transfer of membership letter stating that we were "a member in good standing." All of those transfer letters but mine were accepted without question. My problem was that Quakers teach, as Jesus did, about "baptism of the Spirit" and they do not practice water baptism. I was told that I'd have to be baptized with water in order to be accepted into full membership. Perhaps that was a reasonable requirement, but it felt like a slap in my faith. Did they not consider me a Christian because I was a Quaker?

I carried that question for years wishing for someone who was neither Quaker nor Anabaptist who could hear and help me explore the issue of baptism without needing to convince me one way or the other.

I learned about spiritual direction at a couple of retreats and pastors' weekends at our seminary and was interested, but I didn't know any spiritual directors close to home.

Later, I saw an ad for Shalem Institute for Spiritual Guidance in Washington, D.C. That was another "God thing" where it seemed that I was receiving help from beyond myself. I wrote for more information.

In no time at all, Dr. Gerald May, well-known author and

leader at Shalem, responded with a postal card saying that he had just been in Bluffton to bury his mother beside his father who had died years earlier while serving as a Methodist pastor in another small town nearby.

I applied to Shalem and was accepted in their two-year program with Dr. May as my supervisor. Most of the program required lots of reading at home and writing some papers, but it also included a 10-day retreat of workshops, contemplation, and worship on the Washington, D.C., campus each of the two years. The whole program was a nourishing experience for me.

In order to be a participant, I had to be receiving and providing spiritual direction locally and be accountable to a peer group of directors. I had no idea how to find a director, a peer group, or the two directees that were requirements but I was only mildly surprised as solutions began to unfold.

I was president of the Bluffton Ministerial Association at the time; so, I asked if any of these local pastors knew of spiritual directors or of such a peer group. None did.

A week or so later, a co-pastor at the Presbyterian Church saw me at the gas station at the corner of College Avenue and Main Street. She had remembered that the head of their Presbytery in Findlay had briefly mentioned spiritual direction in the past and she thought he might know more. Indeed, he did.

I investigated and it turned out that he was more than interested in spiritual direction. He had periodically taken personal retreat time at the Catholic Retreat Center in Carey, OH, and he knew that the Sister there would be interested in the peer group that I wanted to establish. The two of them had spoken of the need for some sort of support group but didn't know just how to get one off the ground. Shalem had provided me with the resources for effective structure and procedure.

This key Sister knew some other Catholic Sisters that would

be interested. Thus the peer group was established and we met at the Carey Retreat Center for several years. The group has gone through many member changes due to some being called to and from other parts of the country. Over the years, new participants in the Shalem program have been directed to meet with us as well.

Twenty-eight years later we are now meeting at The Pines Retreat Center in Fremont, OH. The group provides accountability and prayer support, as well as inter-denominational friendship and the opportunity for personal sharing. Many times as I make the hour and a half drive to Fremont, I find myself singing hymns of joy and gratitude. And if I'm not singing, I am likely to be praying for my directees, family, and friends.

Shalem helped me find the pastor of a Methodist Church in Marion, OH. He was in the second year of Shalem's Spiritual Guidance Program and they agreed that he could serve as my director. I drove to Marion once a month to see him.

As for finding the two directees required for me to get started, I put a short article in the MennoLife, our church newsletter. One of our members told a Methodist widow acquaintance about my new project and that widow became my first directee. Three other members of our church also decided to explore what it was like to be in spiritual direction. Another early significant Mennonite relationship in direction was with a friend who was facing cancer and death. Others who came later were driving from Cincinnati, Columbus, Toledo, Ft. Wayne, Wapakoneta, Lockport, and Lima.

I didn't know how to find those connections, but God took control. Some, I realize, would call it all happenstance. I don't.

In retirement, a few of my directees are from my own church who have personal issues they want to explore with someone who will listen without judgment. Others are pastors from a variety of denominations including Lutheran, Presbyterian, and Methodist churches --mostly from outside of Bluffton. They recognize the value of setting aside time to focus on their own spiritual lives, their calling, and various other dreams and "God thoughts." All appreciate a relaxed, compassionate, contemplative, and confidential setting.

Cleansing Prayer

Just God, expressed
in gentle Jesus,
Old Soul of the Eternal
living through Love
forever renewed,
help us to recognize
Your Spirit as it beckons,
and calls us to empty out
our secret sins,
and hurts within.
Fill us with forgiveness,
peace and praise
to pray and sing.
Bless our grace-washed souls
again.

Healing God, expressed
through Jesus,
the One who knows
our human need,
lift our eyes,
fill our longing.
Touch our hope-filled lives
again.

Questions for Individual Reflection and or Group Sharing

1. What experience(s) have you had where you needed to or were required to find a new path? Is/was family support readily available to you?

2. Share faith practices (traditions or rituals) that have been deeply meaningful to you at certain points in your life –times when God has seemed especially present or responsive and involved.

3. Are there issues of doctrine, creed, or religious practice that make you uncomfortable, with which you disagree, or that you need to give more consideration?

4. With whom do you talk when you have issues you need to explore in a confidential setting?

chapter 12

Preparing for the Future

Earlier I wrote about the buy-out of Triplett Corporation, where my husband had been employed for a number of years, by Penril. Stan's instinct told him that he would undoubtedly need to look for other employment and he was concerned about having no pension plan in place. Our two children were adults and off on their own. I had cut back to working part-time; so, Stan's practical concern about funding for retirement came up for serious consideration.

He made an appointment with a financial planner. While we always planned our budget together, Stan always paid the bills and balanced the checkbook. Numbers were never my thing. I don't know how he selected a planner; I just know that she was the wife of a Methodist minister.

I trusted Stan to be thinking about our retirement years and I saw no reason not to trust her. She wanted both of us to be present for our planning sessions. Stan always sat fully alert at her desk during our making-a-plan consultations while I usually sat near the wall –admittedly uncomprehending and a bit bored. Things got interesting though when our plan was complete.

She asked, "Stan, have you ever thought about being a financial advisor? You ask all the right questions and are obviously quite interested in this process." I was surprised and enlightened when he responded that indeed he had thought about it.

The company at that time was called IDS (Investors Diversified Services). The name was later changed to American Express Financial Services and even later to Ameriprise Financial Services. But it was our lady financial advisor who put him in touch with the proper people at IDS and got him started on the path to his final and most satisfying career.

Preparation to become a financial advisor included lots of study which he did in the evenings at home and on the road while traveling to trade shows in various parts of the country as the advertising manager for Triplett prior to its buy-out and then for Penril. While trade-show participants partied in the evenings or simply explored the cities where the trade shows were held, Stan was in his hotel room studying. I don't remember how many tests he had to pass prior to the biggie for licensing, but I know that, like many others, he missed the necessary passing score for licensing by one point the first time he took that all-important final test. He studied still more, then took it again.

In the meantime, we'd been wondering about where he would set up an office. This was certainly a matter of prayer for me and I'm certain that it was for Stan as well. Office space in our small town seemed to be completely occupied. One afternoon we were slowly driving down Main Street trying to imagine where he could possibly set up an office. An attorney whose main office was in Lima, rented space right beside the theater from his brother. That attractive office had a large picture window facing Main Street. There was a small lobby waiting room, storage room, hallway and a small office directly behind the main office. I asked Stan to pull over to the curb and asked him to go in and inquire if that small back room might be available. What happened after that seemed nothing less than a miracle.

The attorney told Stan that he'd been thinking of spending less time in Bluffton and more in Lima. He asked Stan to wait a day or two while he gave this more consideration, and he undoubtedly talked with his brother. When the attorney got back to Stan, he said that if Stan would like to rent the whole space from his brother, he would rent the small room in back from Stan, planning to use it just once a week. That way Stan could have the front office. There could not have been a more perfect offer. Of course Stan agreed.

Stan was so certain that he was next on the list of employees to be let-go at Penril that he'd been slowly bringing his personal items home. At one point he laughingly told me he needed to take some things back in so he could continue working.

He was still waiting for the results of the second licensing test when he had a trade show in St. Louis. Stan's new Penril supervisor was traveling with him this time. Stan suspected it was so he could learn about the nuts and bolts of Stan's job. It is important to note that no one at Penril knew that Stan was already preparing for a new career.

Stan was having dinner with one of the reps following a day at the trade show when she asked, "Who is it that's going to be let go from your office this weekend?" Stan laughed. He knew that this rep had taken the Penril supervisor to dinner the night before.

"It couldn't be anyone but me," Stan replied. Of course he told me about that encounter when he arrived back home. The next day was Friday and he was fully expecting to be let-go. But Friday afternoon the supervisor was still quizzing him about how he handled all aspects of the company's advertising. The inquisition (or information gathering) was still going on well after the office closed and Stan was still an employee.

When he got home, we sat on the front porch and talked while he opened his mail. In it was notification that he had passed the licensing test and was now ready to move ahead. We were thrilled.

I said playfully, "Are you going to tell Penril to take your job and shove it?" To which Stan wisely replied, "No, I don't believe in burning bridges."

Before Stan left for work on Monday morning I said, "When you are let-go I want you to come to my office at the church right away because I want to hear it from you, not from anyone else." He promised he would.

At about 10:00 a.m. he was in my office. He'd been in his office at the former Triplett Corporation when his Penril supervisor stopped at his door and announced, "I need to see you, but I've got to go to the Men's Room first." When he returned, he handed Stan the freshly typed dismissal paper that cryptically said, "Your position has been terminated as of this date."

Stan collected what few personal belongings were still in the office and was escorted out of the building. As such dismissals go, Stan wasn't even permitted time to tell his friends and co-workers goodbye. The reason? It is always a downer for other employees to see their co-workers being dismissed.

It's never fun to be let-go either, but Stan and I both smiled and marveled at the confluence of events. I asked Stan what he was going to do with the rest of his "day-off." He quickly replied, "I'm going to clean the carpet in my new office."

Stan worked happily at financial planning in that office on Bluffton's Main Street for another sixteen years. It was a career that truly suited him. He was nearly 70 when he needed to retire due to health issues. Then he was most fortunate to be able to sell his business to the capable younger man who had been working with and learning from Stan for a couple of years. During those training years, this future owner usually used the small back office because the attorney seldom needed it.

Questions for Individual Reflection and or Group Discussion

1. Have you sensed God's providence in your own or a loved one's employment opportunity? Do you think "gut instinct" is a kind of inner wisdom from God?

2. Have you received guidance beyond your own knowing as you've needed to solve other issues in your world?

3. How well matched are/were your responsibilities with your attained or natural gifts?

4. Have you experienced a time when you felt God was taking far too much time in opening doors?

chapter 13

Seeking to Be a Channel of God's Providence for Others

Spiritual formation begins early in a child's life and charitable living and giving play an important part. Stan's parents were generous supporters of their church, its institutions, and many other worthy causes as well.

> ***Bring the full tithes into the storehouse, that there may be food in my house; and thereby put me to the test, says the Lord of hosts, if I will not open the windows of heaven for you and pour down for you an overflowing blessing.***
>
> **--Malachi 3:10 RSV**

My mother, in spite of being a single parent and always having to wonder if there would be more month than money, always gave ten percent of her income to the work of God's kingdom. There was an envelope marked "Tithe" in her cupboard and it always got paid first whenever money came in.

Since Quakers had no paid ministers, no Sunday morning offering was taken; all meeting expenses were covered by a division of costs between the members. Mother responded to the American Friends Service Committee's request to assist with their work among the needy at home and abroad. She also had a soft heart for some radio evangelists, especially the Billy Graham ministries. If she knew of anyone who had come upon unexpected hard times, Mother would write a note and enclose some money.

When Stan and I were married, we agreed that we would also budget a specified portion of our income for the church and charitable giving. We aimed to be a tithing family, but for the first couple of years when our income was so minimal and our living expenses so fixed, we found that our church pledge of six percent was where we'd need to begin. Then we would work up to ten percent as soon as we could.

Stan created a large ledger with columns for each category of projected spending such as tithe, rent, utilities, insurance, savings and such. Each month we put budgeted cash into separate envelopes for food, gas, and car maintenance. I'm looking at Stan's old records as I write this, and all that was left for miscellaneous spending each month was $1.40. I note that one month that whole amount went for shoe repair. The $10.00 a month allocated for savings nearly always got used up in some account that went slightly over budget.

As our income increased, we achieved our intended goal of tithing and could sometimes give more. It was our planning and frugality plus Stan's careful record keeping that kept us solvent. Needless to say, most of our entertainment was homemade and inexpensive. A few times when we needed a temporary loan to purchase a big item like a newer used car, we borrowed from his life insurance policy or from his parents.

I've written about our careful budgeting in order to set up this next story.

Our fledgling church in Fort Wayne was basically made up of

young couples and lots of babies. The oldest couple was in their forties and had children in high school. We eagerly welcomed new members from the surrounding community, and one such family that had found a home among us had four children. The mother and those children attended regularly, and I knew them well from their participation in Sunday school and Summer Bible School.

We'd never had a funeral in our little congregation and all of us at Maplewood Mennonite Church were quite unprepared for the news one morning that the father of that family had suddenly dropped dead of a heart attack at the gas station where he worked.

We all knew that family struggled to make ends meet and I knew how tight our budget was with only two children to support. I couldn't imagine how they were going to manage now that their head of household was gone. My heart ached for them. As I paced in prayer, I tried to think what I would say when I went over to their house, and I wondered about what food to fix and take. But that all seemed too little to express the depth of my caring. I thought of the bills they would be facing and I assumed that they would have no better means of paying them than we would if this were to happen to our family.

The only discretionary money I had was in an envelope tucked beneath undies in my dresser drawer. It was cash I'd collected a few dollars at a time which Mother had sent for my birthday and which I'd received from selling a few articles and poems. It was enough for only a course or two at the IU-Purdue Extension, but I was squirreling it away with the dream of earning more credit toward a college degree. There was no leeway in our carefully honed budget for continuing my education. Our tithe was already pledged, so I was not free to draw from that account.

Slowly but clearly, I began to realize that I needed to give my personal savings to the family that was hurting. "But *all* of it, Lord?" How could I give away my dream of going back to school?

"*All* of it, Ruth. It's not nearly enough to pay the bills they'll have, but they'll need money now. It's the way they'll know you care."

God's argument in my mind was convincing. I put the cash in another envelope with a note and delivered it along with a casserole for their dinner that night.

In no way was I putting God to a test of generosity nor did I think God was putting me to a test. I simply had a powerful desire to help the family.

Little did I know at that time that we soon would be led back to Bluffton where I could resume work toward my undergraduate degree –and that much of it would be tuition free while Stan was employed at the college. This turned out to be worth much more than the "college nest-egg" I'd given away.

There is a surprising afterglow to this story. At least it was a big surprise to me!

I had already been teaching for a few years at Bluffton High School when a new superintendent was hired.

He smiled broadly when he met me one day saying, "I know something about you that you don't know I know." He proceeded to tell me that someone in the school district he'd just left told him about me when she heard he was moving to Bluffton. She gave him my name and told him about my having given her and her family all the money I'd saved for my further education at the time of her first husband's death. She had remarried and moved from Ft. Wayne to the central Ohio town where he had been superintendent prior to his move to Bluffton. I had lost track of her and her family, but I was reminded that we live in a small world.

I have been the recipient of God's great goodness in so many ways in my lifetime! How could I help but want to help others?

Even though Stan's family financial situation was not as dire as mine when we were students in the early 1950's, we were both recipients of college scholarships. As our income increased we wanted to pay that opportunity forward. We began contributing to financial aid programs for students at Olney Friends Boarding School and at Bluffton College.

During Elmer Neufeld's tenure as college president, Bluffton alumni were challenged to consider establishing and funding scholarships in order to assure that future students can get the kind of education that meant so much to us. Even the U.S. government cooperates with this provision by making the contributions tax-deductible because we as donors do not determine which students receive the aid. We have contributed annually to increase the funds available and we usually receive a thank-you from the student our specific scholarship has helped in each particular year.

There are ways, though, of being a channel of God's provision for others that don't deal with just sharing financial resources. Even before I became a pastor, I was involved with pastoral care. I just didn't think of it that way.

Paul and Ada Wenger were an elderly missionary couple who had retired in Bluffton after serving many years in India. Ada and I first met when we were invited to serve together on a panel about prayer at one of our district conferences.

During this couple's time in India, they had become friends with E. Stanley Jones, the man whose books had helped to shape my spiritual growth. (I wrote earlier about attending an ashram that he led at Lake St. Mary's when I was still living in Ft. Wayne.)

After Stan and I moved to Bluffton, Ada and I developed a spiritual friendship in spite of the significant difference in our ages. Paul had developed health issues that made it difficult for them to get around.

When they learned that E. Stanley Jones was back in the States again and was scheduled for another ashram at Lake St.

Mary's, they wanted to go. I was still teaching, but since they could no longer drive, I said I'd take them to the evening service.

Ada told me that Paul's reason for wanting to attend was for healing prayer, but he was concerned that he would not be able to stand back up after kneeling at the altar. All three of us knew that Ada was not strong enough to help him. Without giving it a second thought I said, "If he wants to go forward, I'll go with him and help him."

I understood his desire for healing but it seemed a bit unrealistic at his age. Nevertheless, I followed through with my promise and as I helped him stand after E. Stanley Jones had "laid hands on him" it was clear to me that he'd not been healed. He'd obviously hoped for a lot from God. I felt so sorry for him and thought what disappointment he must feel. The drive back to Bluffton that night seemed very long to me. I walked them up to their front door. Both thanked me warmly, and then Paul turned to give me a feeble hug. I still remember the surprise I felt as he humbly said, "I was healed tonight." What a lesson for me! Healing is not always visible.

Several months later I heard that they were both in the hospital. Paul was on the main floor and Ada was on the lower level receiving care for depression. They had no family in the area and they were facing dire circumstances. Nevertheless, the man's remarkable faith came through as from memory he quoted verses from the end of Habakkuk:

> ***Though the fig tree do not blossom, nor fruit be on the vines, the produce of the olive fail and the fields yield no food, the flock be cut off from the fold and there be no herd in the stalls, yet I will rejoice in the Lord, I will joy in the God of my salvation. God, the Lord, is my strength;***

he makes my feet like hinds' feet, he makes me tread upon my high places.

-- Habakkuk 3:17-19 RSV

What a testimony!

Before leaving, I asked if there was anything I could do for him. He responded, "There's nothing right now, but if you come back in a couple of days, there might be something you can do." Two days later I went directly to the hospital when my classes were over. He had just died. He had been such a quiet man, but his life still speaks to me.

Another time while I was teaching at Bluffton High School, God tapped me on the shoulder offering another way to assist with caring here on earth. One of my high school students had attracted my attention early on because she seemed to be considerably shyer than many of her classmates. I also noted a sadness in her demeanor and suspected that her home life was not conducive to the sort of self-confidence most of the other girls expressed.

Half-way through her senior year she told me that her parents were separating; they were in financial straits and moving out of the area. She was going to have to live with an aunt and blind grandmother in a town, about fifty miles away. This meant that she would have to change schools and would not be able to graduate with her classmates. My heart told me that I should invite her to live with me and my family for the remainder of the year. I talked with the guidance counselor for more information and advice.

Our Kim was in college, living in a dorm, and this young lady could use Kim's room at home. The grandmother and aunt were already living in crowded quarters and they easily, probably even gratefully, gave her permission to stay in Bluffton if that was what she wanted to do.

Do I think Stan and I were a part of God's providence for this eighteen-year-old? Yes, I do. As I considered what it would mean to our family to take her in, I remembered the special concern I had felt as I first learned to know her as a freshman. I cared for all of my students; so, how was my feeling about this one different? Even now, I don't really know. I just know that I wasn't surprised when she was a senior, and I felt I needed to be involved in ways that exceeded the usual teacher-student relationship.

Yet another time, God showed the way for transition in the church and beyond. After working with our lead pastor at Bluffton's First Mennonite Church for around ten years, he announced his resignation and plan to move. I really wanted to quit working as well, but agreed to stay on as part of the interim pastoral staff. I was not qualified to be a lead pastor and had no desire to be in that position.

I'd often heard other Mennonite women in ministry claim that there were simply no large congregations who were willing to employ a woman as their lead pastor even if she was well-qualified. I thought it was time for that to change. But how does life-giving change happen? Our church was seeking a new leader. Yes, I was praying for wisdom.

While driving alone to our seminary in Elkhart, IN, for the January Pastors' Week, I was thinking about our church's need when a potentially perfect solution came together in my mind. (It was like a light suddenly came on.) I knew that the seminary dean was retiring and I'd worked with the assistant dean, Dorothy Nickel Friesen, in planning for Pastors' Week the previous year. She was in charge of the event again this year. I knew her to be a gifted leader who had previously served well as pastor of a small congregation prior to being called to work at the seminary. Surely the upcoming change in the dean's office must be on her mind and causing her to think about her own future. I was not on our church's pastoral search team and I had no right to speak on their behalf. How could I just check to see if she would even consider changing back to being a full-time pastor?

It turned out to be a rather tumultuous pastor's week because the main speaker was called away for an emergency at home. Dorothy, as chair of the Planning Committee, did a fine but harrowing job of pulling things together. There was no good time for me to talk privately with her even if I had the right to speak with her about the idea that had come to me. That is until. . .

Pastors' Week had just finished. All were eager to be on their way home. I went back to the chapel to copy some information from the bulletin board. Lo and behold, there was Dorothy alone; she was gathering up left-over hand-outs. I walked over to her and said, "Dorothy, I have just one question." I paused. She gave me her full attention.

"Do you ever wish you were a pastor again?" Her shoulders and whole torso lifted as she took in a deep breath and convincingly exhaled a very audible and frustrated "YES!"

My response was quick and to the point. "That's all I wanted to know. That's all I wanted to know." I turned away and left --eager to get back home and talk to the chairperson of our Search Committee.

In a stroke of luck, I found him the next morning sitting alone and away from the Sunday crowd in fellowship hall. I went to him and said, "I know who our next pastor should be."

He was very non-committal as I proceeded to tell him all that I knew –none of which he or the committee knew. After all, Dorothy was an employee of the seminary. They would have no way of knowing that she might be interested. I had no way of knowing what his committee had been thinking or doing; that was not my business. He just listened and I talked.

I also shared my insight with our Conference Minister. Part of his job was to work with church needs and pastoral placement. I told him about my conversation with Dorothy and added that I wanted to retire in a year or so. This would allow a male associate to be hired, facilitating a renewed gender balance.

It was more than three months before I heard that Dorothy was the Search Committee's candidate for our new lead pastor.

Our Conference Minister was busy planning even farther ahead. He, too, was changing positions and subsequently I was invited to fill his shoes for an eighteen-month interim with administrative responsibility for our six-state district until a permanent replacement could be found. The district's need, my past involvement as district president, and a short-term call that would take me to retirement age could make sense all around –if I was willing to step out in faith again and take the risk of saying "Yes." Thus, my last full-time employment prior to retirement was as Interim Conference Minister for the Central District of Mennonite Church USA.

Addendum: Dorothy Nickel Friesen served First Mennonite Church for a little over seven years and was a beloved pastor –the first woman to serve as lead pastor at FMC. She left to accept a position as Conference Minister for the Western District Conference of MCUSA.

Questions for Individual Reflection and or Group Sharing

1. What did you learn about giving from your family of origin? Do you have a plan for giving?

2. Have there been special experiences of blessing in your life that kindled a desire in you to bless others in the same or similar ways?

3. Do you recognize yourself as a channel for God's presence, love, and providence in the world? Tell of a time when you had the opportunity to serve as a "minister" or servant of God in ways that extend beyond the usual "written-down job description" at your place of work, in the community, or at home?

4. Is prayer a part of the way you seek solutions to needs you see around you?

chapter 14

Praying with or on Behalf of Others

I stood in the hallway of Lutheran Hospital's oncology unit, looking over the patient list in my hand, wondering who I should visit next. I was a student chaplain in Lutheran's Clinical Pastoral Education Program.

The door to the private room in front of me was open and the room seemed unusually dark. The Venetian shade was closed. Neither the room lights nor the television was on.

I knocked gently as I entered and said, "Hello, I'm Ruth Naylor from the chaplain's office. I just stopped in to see how you are doing this afternoon."

Tired, sad eyes looked up at me from the bed. The woman's head was wrapped in a turban-like light blue bandanna --hiding baldness resulting from chemotherapy. She shifted on the pillow and tried to speak. It took major effort for her to respond. Her voice was weak and raspy. "Oh, I'm not doing so well this afternoon, I guess."

Right now, I can see myself standing to her right in the grayness of that room. How I wanted to help her! Obviously, I couldn't help her medically. That's the job for doctors and nurses. I would love to bring a little comfort or sunshine into her life, but one doesn't just slap on a religious Band-Aid or give a shot of positive thinking without experiencing something of a spiritual journey with the patient --however short that journey of sharing might be. I certainly didn't want to say anything that would induce guilt for feeling discouraged or even depressed.

I looked at her, wishing I could involve her in conversation, but the effort it had taken for her to speak left no doubt in my mind that conversation was not a good option. I was tempted to offer to pray, but for some reason right then, that seemed too simplistic. It seemed like it would be a slick way to get me off the hook and out of the room. How could I really be of help? --I asked myself. I was groping. And yes, I was uncomfortable.

"I'm sorry you aren't feeling well," I said to this complete stranger. "It's obvious to me that you don't feel like talking. Is there anything I can do for you?" I waited for her answer.

"Just pray," she whispered.

"I'll be glad to," I replied. My mind was racing ahead. I don't know whether or not she has a family. I don't know what church she belongs to, if any. (Sometimes, knowing the denomination makes a difference in how one prays --or in the religious language one uses.) I don't know whether she hopes to live or die. Oh God, how can I link her significantly to you in a way that you and your presence will remain real to her after I've gone? Clearly, I'm not going to cheer her with this little visit today, but if I could just find a way to hook into whatever faith she has and let that give her a spiritual focus for the future. . ..

I picked up her hand in mine. Suddenly I heard myself saying, "Do you know the Lord's Prayer?" She nodded her head slightly, indicating that she did. There was nothing but weariness in her demeanor.

"I'm going to include the Lord's Prayer as part of my prayer," I said, "and I invite you to either pray it or think it along with me." I don't remember what I prayed extemporaneously, but it wasn't long before I was into the Lord's Prayer. I thought I heard her praying with me, but I wasn't sure. I listened closely so I could set a pace that would honor her ability to stay with me. Suddenly in the distraction of thinking about how she was doing, I realized that I was lost. Yes! Lost in the Lord's Prayer. I thought maybe I'd left out a line. Surely she would miss it. I hesitated for just a moment and then went on to finish as gracefully as I could.

I gave her hand a little squeeze and laid it down on the bed. Feeling a need to acknowledge my blundering in the prayer, I chuckled. "There's one for you to remember," I said. "The chaplain messed up on the Lord's Prayer!" For the first time, I saw her smile.

Half reading her lips and half deciphering her whisper, I heard her say, "That's okay."

"Well," I said, "I hope you have a good day anyway." And I started to move away. She reached her hand toward me and said, "Maybe I'll just have you open the shade for me."

"Sure. Glad to!" And as I went around her bed and to the other side of the room, I tried to explain. "At our church we don't say the Lord's Prayer much anymore. We sing it. One of our members is a composer, and he wrote special music for it. It's really pretty. Goes like this." . . .And I tried to sing it for her. But it didn't sound right. I had never sung it without the special organ introduction that always leads the congregation in singing that particular piece. Without the accompaniment, I didn't know whether I was singing Malotte's version or Bixel's version. It sounded so strange that I stopped, embarrassed again.

By then I had opened the shade and turned around to look at her. Her eyes were sparkling with amusement, and there was a new radiance in her face. The afternoon sunshine flooded the room, baptizing us both with light. She was laughing with me --not at me. She could forgive my human frailty. In that moment I knew the joy of being vulnerable to another. It was good to be human --even to be imperfect.

She pointed at me and said, "I want you to come back and see me again. You be sure you come back."

I learned that day that God can use even imperfect prayers.

On another occasion, I stood at the hospital bed of one of my church members. Ella was in her 90's and just one of so many who, over the years, won my pastor heart. Her eyes were weakly focused beyond those of us who were in the room. She had been refusing food and water for days. It was Good Friday.

Apparently, her life on earth was soon to end. Stories she had told me over the previous four years when I visited her in one of our local nursing homes flooded my mind. Ella, this silver-haired widow, had led a simple but love-filled life. She had worked in a hospital laundry until she was 80 --"just keeping busy." Now she was swathed in sheets similar to those which she had so lovingly folded for others.

My own silent prayer was, "Lord, just take her in your loving arms and carry her home." The next morning I woke early with Ella on my mind. How appropriate, I thought, that Ella could die at Eastertime. Words unfolded in my mind and I wrote them down.

Ella's Easter Morning

The morning has come!
I must call at the tomb.
Somehow I don't really expect
to find her there.
The clothes of death
will be lying empty;
and the room of my heart
will be filled with light,

and hope. --Yes,
and happiness
that she has been released
from her bonds
to walk freely
in the garden.

And in the small hours of that Saturday morning between Good Friday and Easter, I knew that Ella's family members would be re-examining recent days and cherished memories from the past. There were words for that too:

Time for Vacation

Weak old eyes look up from the hospital bed
searching for a familiar face.
They focus somewhere near the ceiling.
"I want to go. I want to go."

It's time to move to a pleasanter clime
where one can live unencumbered
by the snow and ice of winter--
a place where pure sunshine warms the soul.

In the morning there'll be
a newly vacated shell on the beach
and it will be a lovely find. . .
washed beautiful by waves of memory.
We'll tenderly pick it up
and listen for the roar of the sea.

But those poems were premature. Much to everyone's surprise, Ella lingered. The following week, when I visited her, the nurses had her propped up in a chair. "She hasn't been responding to people at all," the head nurse told me, "but you can go in and try."

Ella's eyes were closed. Indeed, she didn't respond. I was about to leave when it struck me that I ought to offer to pray anyway. "Ella, would you like for me to pray the Lord's Prayer with you?"

I thought I saw her nod. I took her hand in mine and began, "Our Father. . . ." Her voice was raspy at first and then became quite clear and firm as she prayed each word, even taking the lead on some phrases. I was amazed. Her eyes remained closed and, as I left, she spoke very softly and as from a distance. "Thank you," she said. "Thank you."

Ella went back to the nursing home and made remarkable improvement. I visited her periodically and would often meet a member of her family either coming or going. Still another Easter came and went.

It was late August when one of Ella's family members saw me on the street and said that Ella was ill again and unresponsive.

I went to see her. The curtain between the two beds in her room was partially drawn when I entered. Her eyes were closed. She looked tiny, thinner than usual. I spoke to her. No response. I had taken my Bible and was prepared to read a Psalm, but somehow that seemed too heavy, too planned. Maybe even too professional.

It seemed foolish to stay when she could not acknowledge my presence. Still, I took her hand in mine and just sat there in silence, wondering what I should do and how long I should stay. It entered my mind to softly sing a hymn or two. But what would her roommate think? I hesitated.

The impulse did not go away. A prayer hymn came to mind and it seemed to fit what I knew to be the desire of Ella's heart. I began to sing softly:

Precious Lord, take my hand,
Lead me on, help me stand,
I am tired, I am weak, I am worn.
Thru the storm, thru the night,
Lead me on to the light,
Take my hand, precious Lord,
Lead me home.

She opened her eyes wide with a wondering look. Where was that song coming from? Softly, she said, "Yes. Oh yes, Lord."

When the song was finished, I paused, wondering what I should sing next. She closed her eyes. Then I began the familiar "What a Friend We Have in Jesus." At ninety-five, Ella's voice was scratchy and the tune was almost gone, but her heart knew the music of the words and it was in her to sing. Together we sang those lyrics that have spanned generations. Our hearts were full.

Ella died one week later --on my birthday. Though it was the third of September, I know it was Ella's Easter morning.

And now another story. Praying about the really tough stuff.

> ***In the same way, the Spirit helps us in our weakness. We do not know what we ought to pray for, but the Spirit himself intercedes for us with groans that words cannot express. And he who searches our hearts knows the mind of the Spirit because the Spirit intercedes for the saints in accordance with God's will.***
>
> **--Romans 8:26-27 NIV**

The phone was ringing after midnight. It was the week after Christmas. The day before, at our Sunday worship service, our senior pastor had announced that he'd be away on vacation and that I would be available to handle emergencies. Among other announcements in the Sunday bulletin was this one:

> We extend sympathy and love to the family of Neil and Eileen Kehler. Eileen's brother, Willard Myers, died very unexpectedly on Christmas morning at Quakertown, Pennsylvania. Neil, Eileen, and the children plan to attend funeral services this evening and will probably drive back to Bluffton on Monday afternoon and night. The family would appreciate our prayers.

I turned over in bed and picked up the phone. For months, Neil's trembling voice on the other end of the line would come back to haunt me. "Ruth, we've had a terrible accident. We need you to come immediately." His voice broke with emotion. "Bonnie's dead." He asked me to call someone else and come in two cars. Lots of help would be needed.

All the Kehler children had been my students in high school. I knew them well. Neil gave information about where they were on Route 30 and reported that Eric and Cheryl were still trapped in their crushed car. Emergency vehicles were on their way.

My first instinct was to call and see if our senior pastor might still be in town. He was. But his gas tank was nearly empty and filling stations in our small town weren't open at that hour. Stan and I agreed to pick him up. He called our district conference minister, who also lived in Bluffton, to take a second car and meet us near Williamstown where the accident had occurred. Eileen, Neil's wife and the mother of these children, was the administrative assistant in the district conference office and it seemed appropriate to ask the conference minister to join us.

A half-hour later, as all of us arrived at the scene, we met two ambulances just leaving for the hospital in Findlay. Rescue workers had been unable to gain access to the injured young people until they sent for the "jaws of life," and now after a prolonged wait, the two young people were on the way to getting medical help. We barely saw their crushed vehicle off the left side of the road or the eighteen-wheeler out in a field on the right. We didn't see the patch of black ice in the road which had spun Eric's car into the path of the truck.

Eileen and Neil, along with a brother and sister-in-law in the back seat of their car, had been following in tandem with Eric's car. Bonnie had chosen to ride up front with Eric after they stopped for something to eat in Columbus. Cheryl had gone to sleep in Eric's back seat. Eileen and Neil hadn't noticed that they'd fallen a bit behind Eric until they ran over a piece of metal in the road. Was that a piece of a car? Could that shadow they glimpsed in the ditch have been a car? They pulled over and stopped. Neil ran back, fear pounding in his heart. He heard the moaning. He saw Bonnie. Dead. (This was before the time of cell phones.) He ran to the nearest house and knocked loudly. No response. Then he saw another house farther away. It was from there that he had called.

There wasn't time to hear the story or ask questions so we turned around and followed the ambulances. The decision at the emergency room was to life-flight Eric to Toledo Hospital as soon as the helicopter could get to Findlay. Again the wait was interminable. All we could do was hold each other. I was too paralyzed with emotion to pray aloud. Yet my mind and heart petitioned over and over "O God. . . ." I felt so utterly helpless.

At one point a nurse came to tell us as gently as she could that we were in danger of losing both Eric and Cheryl. It seemed more than we were willing to imagine. It was just one more blow in that nightmare of a night.

Finally, it was decided that while Eric was being transferred by helicopter, Cheryl would be transported to the Toledo Hospital in an ambulance. Their father, Neil, would go with Stan and me in our car to Toledo. Our senior pastor and conference minister would go back to Bluffton with Eileen and begin funeral plans for Bonnie.

At Toledo in those wee hours of the morning, we waited again while medical personnel in the trauma unit evaluated injuries before beginning any kind of treatment or surgery. Eventually, Neil and I were invited to join them in the trauma room. Eric was barely recognizable. His body was crushed and broken in numerous places. Severe lacerations in his face and near his left eye looked ominous. He was unconscious most of the time, but he occasionally responded to our calling his name or asking him to squeeze the hand that was holding his. It was clear that the emergency workers believed he might die at any moment and that even if he did survive, permanent brain damage was likely.

Cheryl's back was broken in four places; her surgery would wait until the next day.

The hospital chaplain, who was on call for emergencies that night finally arrived and, amidst the bustle of doctors and nurses, asked if we'd like him to pray. Neil looked at me and surprised me when he replied, "No, I guess not." He took my hand and squeezed it, adding, "I think God knows the prayer of our hearts." Surely each of us wanted whatever would be best for Eric, Cheryl, and the family in the long run, and none of us knew what that was.

For the next twenty-four hours, we ran on energy we didn't know we had. Cheryl's husband, who had been at home with their children, found care for them and came to join us as we waited through surgery that could either be very successful or leave her paralyzed. "Oh God, stand with Cheryl, the doctors and nurses . . .and all of us in this difficult time."

Cheryl came out of her surgery to spend extended time in a circle bed (like a hamster wheel) while her spine healed around the rods which would eventually enable her to walk. Cheryl, a nurse by profession, suffered a great deal of pain and inconvenience, but was surrounded by friends, family, medical personnel, pastors, and prayers that provided support --not only to her, but to her husband and children as well. It became clear that she would recover.

Eric had surgeries to correct compound fractures and multiple internal injuries. His coma was medically deepened to keep the swelling in his brain from causing seizures and further damage.

On my way to Toledo to visit Eric one day, I pulled off the side of the highway to write a prayer that I could leave for him to find, if and when he came out of his coma, so he would know that his friends had been praying for him. But just in case he could hear in his subconscious state, I prayed aloud at his bedside as well. I wanted to reassure him of his link to God, and I knew now what I wanted to say to God. Eric made no visible response to my being there, but I hoped he had heard my prayer. I knew God had heard.

There was no nightstand beside his bed in the Intensive Care Unit and I could see no place to leave my written prayer. I decided to bring it on home with me and put it under a small file box on my desk. Twelve years later, it was still there.

This is the prayer:

> *Our Father God, we know that you love us and that you are with us at all times, and in all places. Hold Eric's hand and lead him in love to wholeness of body, mind, and spirit. We pray in the name of Jesus. Amen.*

I believe that even as we walk through and beyond the valley of the shadow of death, our Good Shepherd is with us. Whether we live or whether we die, we are the Lord's if we have faith to believe and trust that grace-filled Truth. The thought underlying my written prayer was meant to cover either life as we know it here on Earth or the wholeness of being in Heaven. The place of wholeness was left up to God.

There were long months of recovery and healing, but many years later, I can report that both Eric and Cheryl are well and living very productive lives.

As a pastor I was often invited to pray on public occasions not related to the church. Some were a joy, such as praying at my former students' commencement ceremony the year following my resignation as a teacher.

I was usually asked to offer the mealtime prayer at the American Express/Ameriprise annual Christmas banquet. My husband's boss, who was usually very appreciative, qualified his request the last year that he was in charge of the party.

"You'll want to keep the prayer short and to the point of just giving thanks because we don't want to offend our new financial planner who is Jewish." I gave special thought to his request but decided that I could use language that was sensitive to both Jewish and Christian faiths. Here is that prayer. As you can see, it wasn't particularly short. I wanted to include thoughts about serving with Love:

> *Eternal God of Light and Love, we acknowledge your Life among us here this evening, and we thank you for the blessings of yet another year. We are grateful for work to do –and for a company that calls its employees to serve others in the same manner as they themselves would like to be served. Indeed, as the Messiah is prophesied in Scripture, your people are reminded to do justice, to love mercy, and to walk humbly with you. May we indeed, be your*

servant people. Let your Light continue to direct and protect us in this Holiday season and throughout the New Year ahead.

Just now, we thank you for this food and the opportunity for fellowship around these tables –that both body and soul might be nourished and blessed together. We pray these things in the Spirit of your Love which is forever made visible among us in deeds of justice, love, and compassion. Amen.

There was another time when I was quite conscious of needing to think beyond the circle of my own Christian tradition. I was president of the Bluffton Ministerial Association when a Japanese business (DTR) built a lovely new facility here. They planned a Shinto service as part of a grand opening celebration such as our community had never seen. I received a formal personalized invitation not only to attend but to provide an invocation. Although I could not find a copy of that prayer, I did need to think broadly (as does the poem that follows) in order to include all of God's children.

Abstraction

"In the beginning was the ***Word***!"
That's what the Scripture says.
"The Word was in the beginning
and the Word was ***God***." Indeed.
Scripture also says that God is ***Love***.

So surely, the Word, in the beginning,
was Love. Somehow it got separated
by distraction from Eden's lexicon

until that Word came to dwell among us
clothed in human flesh, offering
a grace-filled word-free demonstration.
Even though its definition gets distorted,
it offers transformation, even resurrection
in the everyday prose of living.

Breathe again among and in us, Holy Spiritus,
translate and write your Word in human hearts.
Arrange our discouraged world into a poem.

Questions for Individual Reflection and or Group Sharing

1. Have you ever made a mistake that turned out to be a blessing? Or to state it another way, how have you learned that you don't have to be perfect?

2. Have you ever wanted to encourage a loved one who was quite ill or dying by reminding them of your shared faith?

3. Have you ever been in a traumatic situation where you simply couldn't pray or when you felt confused about how to pray?

4. Have you been in circumstances where your faith culture's view of God has been invited or challenged to expand or evolve into new understandings?

chapter 15

Dealing Personally with Death

December 1956: Ligonier, Indiana

Standing at the kitchen sink in the dark, I pressed my pregnant belly against the countertop and reached up into the cupboard for the familiar round pharmacist's bottle which contained mineral oil. I felt the familiar pint in my hand, screwed off the cap, and took a big slug directly from the bottle trying to get it as far back in my throat as possible so I wouldn't have to feel it in my mouth or taste it. Immediately I began to choke, and the familiar odor of carbon tetrachloride announced my deadly mistake.

Several months earlier while still living in Indianapolis, I had complained to my gynecologist about being constipated. The nightly dose of mineral oil at bedtime was his recommended solution and I had purchased that pint at Methodist Hospital where I worked. Being employed in the superintendent's office at the time, I was eligible for a discount on anything purchased in the hospital pharmacy.

During my two years there, I had also picked up a pint of carbon tetrachloride to use as a spot remover. This miracle solvent saved on dry-cleaning bills. I had never thought about the fact that the mineral oil and the carbon tetrachloride were in exactly the same kind of bottles with exactly the same kind of labels --except for the typewritten words on each label which spelled out the contents.

That fall, my husband and I moved to northern Indiana and rented a duplex. He had a new job. We were fixing up a nursery and eagerly anticipating our first child, due in January. One thing that bothered me about our new home was a fairly large grease spot on the wallpaper in the living room.

Our mothers being the helpful sort gave us advice about many things. "Do you have any cleaning fluid?" my mother asked. "I might be able to get that unsightly spot off the wallpaper." I produced the bottle of carbon tetrachloride, and sure enough. With Mother's gentle patience, it worked beautifully. The spot was completely gone.

My mother-in-law heard what we had used to remove the greasy spot and remembered an article which she had read in a current issue of *Readers' Digest* about the deadly dangers of that same widely used spot remover. She insisted that I read the article and that I take special precautions with the carbon tetrachloride.

It sounded like a wise idea, but I obviously wasn't as concerned as she, because when she asked me a couple of weeks later if I'd read the article I said, "I must admit that I haven't. You already told me what it says." I could see her disappointment, and I quickly added, "But I do plan to look it up and read it."

"Frankly, I think you should just get rid of that stuff. It's too dangerous to have around the house," she mused.

Her suggestion seemed like exaggerated concern to me. After all, both my husband and I were responsible people, and we were far too thrifty to throw away anything useful.

However, with that second prompting, I did look up the article and was amazed at some of the horror stories it reported. I told Stan about the article, and we agreed that our bottle of cleaning fluid should be kept out on a high shelf above our laundry equipment on the enclosed back porch.

How the carbon tetrachloride ever got into the kitchen cupboard is a mystery. But there was no doubt in my mind about what I had just swallowed that December night. I was standing wide awake in a nightmare, gagging, spitting, choking --hardly able to breathe.

Stan, in his pajamas, was immediately beside me. I ordered him to go read the *Digest* article. I rinsed out my mouth and raced to the phone to call the doctor. Surely, he would tell us to drive to a hospital emergency room and have my stomach pumped.

This small-town general practitioner, who had taken me on as his patient after we left the trusted gynecologist/obstetrician in Indianapolis with whom I'd begun my prenatal care, seemed far more laid-back than I thought he should be. I knew we were in dire circumstances. And after quickly scanning the article, Stan knew it too.

"Force yourself to vomit," my doctor was saying on the phone, "and then drink cream."

"I've already tried to vomit and I couldn't," I barked helplessly, "and we don't have any cream in the house." I was frustrated that he wasn't any more concerned than he seemed to be. I didn't have to tell him that no local stores would be open at 10:30 at night. He'd lived in that small town a lot longer than we had.

"Well, stick a spoon handle down your throat until you vomit. And if that doesn't work, drink some very salty water. That should accomplish it." He went on in his quiet, untroubled way. He must have had on his pajamas too. "You probably didn't actually swallow very much. When you choked, you undoubtedly spit most of it out. Do you have any condensed milk?"

"I've got a can of Carnation. Is that what you mean?"

"Yes. Drink that. The whole can. It should counter the petroleum in the carbon tet."

I hung up the phone and went back to the kitchen sink. I tried the spoon handle while Stan fixed salt water for me. Nothing worked. Knowing that it was supposed to work, Stan decided I wasn't doing it right.

At my left side his voice turned from compassionate concern to authoritative command, "Stick that spoon handle farther down your throat. You've got to vomit." Then he sympathetically began to gag for me and promptly went into the bathroom and vomited in the stool.

Drinking pure Carnation condensed milk was enough to make me upchuck under ordinary circumstances, but I managed to get it down. Finally, we had done all we knew to do and we went to bed exhausted.

We kissed goodnight as usual, and I'm sure Stan figured we'd done the best we could. We had followed Doctor's orders. If there was more that we needed to be worrying about, he would have sent us to the hospital.

As I lay there thinking about what had happened and what would surely be the outcome, tears silently slipped from my eyes and soaked my pillow. I wasn't afraid to die. I felt personally safe in God's care. But I felt so sorry for Stan. In my mind's eye, I could see myself, eight months pregnant with his child, lying dead in a casket. All this, just two weeks before Christmas. How would he cope with the death of his wife and his unborn baby whom he'd already grown to love?

If I should die before I wake? "I'm yours, God. But do stay near to Stan as he goes through these next days and weeks." Even as I prayed, I was burping carbon tetrachloride –a most unpleasant taste.

In no time at all, I was asleep. It wasn't until morning that I realized just how certain I was that I would die in the night. It was the only time in my life that I have been truly surprised to find myself awake.

Sunshine was streaming into our room, but the yukky vaporous taste was still in my mouth –an ugly reminder of the previous night.

January 1957: Lagrange, Indiana

This next brief story might reveal something about my subconscious state of mind, at the time this first child was born, particularly as it relates to motherhood and the end of life.

On January 25, 1957, six weeks after the carbon tetrachloride episode, I was in the delivery room at the Lagrange, Indiana, hospital which was a half-hour away from our home in Ligonier. I had earlier informed my doctor, and I told the nurse on duty that night, that I wanted to experience natural childbirth as nearly as possible. I certainly did not want a general anesthetic. Ether was commonly used in those days, but I wanted to be conscious so I could experience the whole miracle of birth.

Everything progressed rapidly and my doctor did not arrive until I was in the very last stages of labor. I remember seeing him come in the delivery room door. He was casually smoking a cigar prior to washing his hands at the sink. The attending nurse was getting impatient. With real urgency in her voice she said, "Doctor, you've got to get over here. She's going to tear."

He confidently commanded, "Put her out."

The nurse obediently placed a mask over my nose and mouth and said, "Breathe deeply." I turned my head to get away from the mask and she said, "If you don't want it, just blow it away." In an effort to blow it away, I took a couple of really deep breaths and was out.

Two hours later I began to regain consciousness. It was in the twilight prior to full consciousness that I had a dream I'll never forget.

I was standing in a tunnel filled with a long line of women. One at a time beginning from the far end of the tunnel, each woman in turn was saying with labored effort, "I am the next, to the next, to the next, to the next, to the. . .happiest woman in the world." It took effort for each woman to make her statement and each one dropped off one more of the "next to. . ." qualifying phrases.

I wondered how many of "the next's" I'd still need to include by the time it was my turn to speak. Eventually I heard, "I am the next to the next to the happiest woman in the world." I realized that the woman right beside be would be saying, "I am the next to the happiest woman in the world." It was then that I realized I was the one who was left to say, "I am the happiest woman in the world."

My life-long dream of being both a wife and mother had come true. With my loving husband and the baby I had not yet seen, I felt that I truly was the happiest woman in the world. **But** in that dream, I also knew that as soon as I said my line, the ether bubble that we were in and that made it so hard to speak, would burst. And **it would be the end of the world.** It was okay. I was sad about life being over, but I couldn't imagine a more wonderful way for the world to end.

I spoke my part in the dream and was suddenly conscious with Stan at my bedside. I was vomiting as a result of too much ether.

The nurse had taken our baby back to the nursery. She wasn't very happy when I insisted that she bring her back and unwrap her so I could count her perfect little fingers and toes.

2001-2015: Bluffton, Ohio.

In July of 2001 Stan began waking in the night soaked with sweat even though our house was air conditioned. He also mentioned cloudy vision in one eye. When he complained one night of having chest pain, I insisted that he make an appointment for a complete physical.

Stan's general practitioner was concerned about the night sweats and wanted to check that out while ordering other routine tests. When the reports came back, the PSA was seriously elevated and we began planning for prostate surgery. Facing cancer led me to realistically consider the possibility of losing Stan and what that would mean for him as well as for me.

Until 2001, except for the early incident with carbon tetrachloride, we were not concerned about our mortality because we'd always enjoyed good health. We did have to consider and help to make decisions about traditional burial or cremation when our parents died. That led to conversation about own demise, but it was always in an academic and practical planning way. Sometimes I thought about my own death in a poetic way as well.

Pre-Planning

When I die
I want my loved ones
to fling my ashes
into the wind.
Sow them
as I've tried to sow
my poems.

I long for freedom.
Don't put me
in a box or urn
to languish on a shelf
or in a grave.

Swing hands high,
arms in an arc above
the Riley bridge.
Let my ashes fly
downstream from
the campus flood plain
where I nearly died,
yet learned to love.

Look to the sky
and do not brood.
Let your hearts
sing when you release me
as Noah loosed the dove.
I'll wing my way
around the written rainbow,
then pluck the promised signs
of life renewed—
the olive branch and peace.

Stan and I completed legal wills as soon as our first child was born and we kept them up to date as our life stages changed. None of us knows when such legal questions might need to be answered because of accident or illness. Early on, we wanted to stipulate who would care for our children if both of us were killed in an accident.

When we moved to Bluffton, our church was encouraging

even young couples like us to complete advanced planning forms, medical directives, power of attorney, etc. It seemed like a wise thing to do and we did it.

After watching the family of one of Mother's sisters take extreme measures to keep their mother medically alive long after she no longer knew them, and even after she had lost consciousness, I knew for certain that I did not want my children to do that to me.

Document This

This medical directive
is a gift I give
to you, my children,
while I am still alive.
I'm not afraid
to look at death.

Love reigns and
has trumped earth's clay.
Eternal arms embrace us
In a mysterious way
that death cannot annul.

Don't you worry
when my ticket comes.
I'll not want a later flight
when I am offered
wings to fly.

I'll love you always
and you know
I'd hate a long goodbye.

I'd always had a running joke with Stan that he was not allowed to die before me because I would be so lost without him to handle our finances and so many of our worldly affairs.

Stan loved life and enjoyed thinking in terms of living, not dying. He planned to work until he was 70. With retirement we wanted to experience a voluntary service assignment abroad, but his medical issues denied us that dream.

While we were preparing for his prostate surgery, it was discovered that he had complicating blood issues. His general practitioner was concerned about hemorrhaging; however, the special surgeon in Columbus assured us that he'd dealt with such things before and was not afraid to proceed.

After the surgery but before we left the hospital in Columbus, they did a bone marrow test and we learned that Stan had chronic lymphocyte leukemia. It was treatable but not curable. Thus our 14 years of dealing with a multitude of Stan's health issues began.

Early on, he was able to enjoy life with the regular medical supervision and care of his oncologist who explained that he was already in stage four of the CLL when diagnosed. It had destroyed his immune system. He had surgery to remove his spleen and to install a double port for various infusions.

In the years that followed, he experienced a variety of complications. Our lives seemed to revolve around other specialists, treatments, and many different prescriptions. At one point, he had kyphoplasty in his spine to hopefully help with his back pain –but it didn't help. None of his physicians could clearly predict the future, but the final outcome was undeniable.

Stan and I enjoyed holding hands and taking walks together for exercise while enjoying the beauty of nature around us. We started out doing the two-mile square in the rural countryside where we lived, but eventually it was all he could do to walk around the block that contained our small housing development beside the local golf-course.

Sometimes I needed to walk alone, and I usually used that time to pray --dumping my worries along the way. Many times, I'd softly sing hymns to keep my thoughts on a higher plane. I liked it whenever a line or two for a new poem would come. This one was just plain fun:

A Walking Prayer

Omniscient God,
help me to be
good, grace-filled, and gracious:
pure without being prissy
dedicated without being a drudge
committed without being cocky
just without being judgmental
fun-loving without being a fool
serious but not stuffy
help me to be
acceptable in your sight--
this side of being an angel.

The time came when Stan's monthly infusions were not enough. He coughed day and night. His back hurt constantly. I was concerned about the prescribed opioids he was receiving. Eventually, I questioned his oncologist about it.

"Do you think he is becoming addicted to the pain medications?" The doctor shook his head and said, "We don't worry about addiction in situations like this."

The following poem reflects on a late autumn vacation when my brother and his wife invited us to join them at Massanutten Resort in Virginia:

Prognosis

This rainy day holds the sunshine
as in mountainous territory
courage and hope walk together—
family history flows behind us.
Nights ahead are forecast to be cold
unseasonably so, but
hand in hand, our path is warmed.

What new scenes are yet to be
discovered as we faithfully exercise
pledged togetherness?
How many new prescriptions wait
to challenge or nourish our souls
when coughed-up questions
speak a foreign tongue?

Words are cherished, but
they are hesitant to convey
feelings and fears deep inside
where initial and lived attraction
has ripened into a partnership
that sustains our world.

The cloud ahead is one
of unknowing. The Spirit, though
often hidden, is ever present.
That and one other thing is certain:
the cemetery where ancestors are
plotted lies ahead and promises
that our future will be together.

My most frequent prayer was one of gratitude to God for the many wonderful years we had shared together.

In December 2014 Stan made plans for a relaxing vacation in May at a timeshare resort in Orlando, Florida. We'd had a good time at that resort two or three years earlier. I worked on putting together my first collection of poems while we were there because Stan was not in shape for a lot of activity. He had simply enjoyed relaxing in the hot tub and at the pool right in front of our unit.

As our get-away time approached in the spring of 2015, I worried that he simply wasn't well enough to make the trip. Besides constant weakness and pain, he was dealing with vertigo, diarrhea and incontinence, plus occasional vomiting, long lasting hiccups, and frequent nosebleeds.

The one encouraging thing was that after years of coughing 24/7 and a couple of bouts with pneumonia, his pulmonary specialist had finally gotten that under control. Stan would, however, need to keep using his vibrating vest and a nebulizer twice a day to deal with the bronchiectasis that had developed.

Although Stan occasionally had a reasonably good day, he was in no shape to drive and I couldn't see how I'd handle driving the whole way myself while trying to meet his needs on the way. I also dreaded the possibility of his having to be hospitalized away from home. I kept praying for wisdom, feeling certain that we should cancel the plans Stan had made. Yet I knew how terribly disappointed he would be if we didn't get to go.

Stan's brother came on Thursday for a two-day visit in Bluffton. I confessed my concern to his wife. Then on Saturday our son Jeff and his wife were in Bluffton. While Nancy attended a shower for one of her nieces and Stan was napping in the recliner, Jeff and I had a good talk on the patio. He understood my concern.

Then I received assistance from those family members who knew my concern. On Sunday morning we received an email from Stan's brother. It was copied to both Kim and Jeff. The message was strongly advising us to fly to Florida. He'd looked up and sent various airline schedules.

At 6:26 A.M. on Monday, Jeff emailed information on another non-stop flight out of Ft. Wayne that was very reasonable. Then Kim and one of her daughters picked up the concern and offered to take us to any of the airports and pick us up when we came home.

Stan and I had considered flying even before these emails arrived. But we knew we simply couldn't manage ourselves in an airplane or airport with all the medical equipment we'd need to take. Flying wouldn't solve our dilemma about the possibility of Stan's needing medical assistance in an unfamiliar place either. However, the support of family members who shared my concern about driving helped make my point.

It was our habit to read the daily devotional in *Rejoice!* magazine every morning at breakfast. And on Monday morning, I was fascinated when the heading for the day's reading was "Stop Talking and Listen." The writer said, "The listening process starts with paying attention to God. . .. The Spirit can also speak to us in quiet, reflective moments or through the wise advice of a trusted friend." And then the responsive prayer at the end was: "Lord, in the midst of many distractions, help me take time to truly hear your voice."

If that wasn't enough, the *Lima News* Lockhorns cartoon that day showed the harried couple wearily carrying vacation luggage with decals that said, "Hell & Back." The Lockhorns' neighbor, noticing their condition, asked, "Rough vacation?"

After a near sleepless Monday night in which I couldn't forget the devotional and the cartoon, I prayed again about the wisdom of going and for a way to let Stan know how worried I was. I knew he'd be very unhappy if I again suggested cancellation.

He'd already packed his bags ready to go. In previous weeks I'd hinted any number of times that I thought we were foolish to try to make this trip, but Stan did not want to hear it. I'd reminded him that he'd miss our recliner for his morning, afternoon, and evening naps –and for use in the night if he couldn't sleep in bed.

I knew I had to say something more. But what? And how?

Tuesday morning, I finally told him that if a directee came to me with family members' concerns, the devotional, and then the cartoon, I'd encourage them to consider whether that might be God speaking to them.

I said that we obviously had our family members concerned about the wisdom of our driving and that we'd be creating a real problem for them as well as for ourselves if anything went wrong or if they had to come and rescue us. I admitted that as much as I was trying to care for him and wanted him to be happy, I thought this added stress could do me in. He walked past me softly muttering that he'd just cancel the trip. He still did not want to admit the seriousness of his condition.

After breakfast, I went to water-aerobics by myself. For months, we had enjoyed that activity together, but now his skin, which was very thin and would tear with the slightest pressure, had three places that were still too raw for him to be in the pool. When I returned, it was obvious that he'd had another bathroom accident. He also told me with disappointment in his voice that he'd cancelled the vacation.

As it turned out, he ended up spending what would have been that whole vacation week in the Findlay Hospital, and that week was followed by ten days in the Mennonite Memorial Home rehab unit. I was so grateful that we weren't in Florida.

Needless to say, it was a difficult summer. Two years earlier, we had down-sized. A granddaughter and her husband had purchased our home place and we moved to Maple Crest, a local retirement community where Stan had no yard care responsibilities.

I observed his physical decline but he still expected things to get better. Falling became a big problem. Because his back hurt so badly, it was difficult to help him get up. The first time, I called for our grandson, Sam, who lived several blocks away, to come help me. We tried to figure out the least painful way to accomplish our goal, then Sam bent down and picked him up in both arms and carried him to his bed. We had two 911 calls following falls that we just couldn't handle, and he ended up in the emergency room and then the hospital both times.

When the time came to consider hospice care, he was slow to recognize or accept that. I'd been living with the specter of his slow death for quite some time and hospice was such welcome help when Stan begged to discontinue physical therapy, during his second rehabilitation stint at MMH. He was too weak and exhausted to continue.

The palliative care doctor we'd met at the hospital was also the hospice doctor. He came to MMH to discuss hospice care. He and I were sitting very close to Stan. The doctor said, "Stan, you are living a medical life. Is that good enough?" I restated the question. "Is this medical life a satisfactory life?" Stan wearily said, "No." It was August 10, 2015 and we changed the paper-work from palliative care to hospice care.

An email to my brother in Georgia the next day says: "Generally I can stay pretty strong. Counting on God's presence provides me with courage to face each day now. But when people give me compassionate hugs, my eyes leak."

Stan wanted me to bring him home from MMH. On the 31st of August, I did. It was hard work because he could no longer walk and I had to help him into and out of a transport chair and push it wherever he wanted or needed to go, but it was a privilege to be at his beckoning call.

At times he still seemed to anticipate getting better. Indeed, after taking him off of all his meds, his mind was clearer and he seemed to feel better too. A number of times, though, he either forgot or just wanted to prove to himself that he could stand and walk. He inevitably fell and I had to call for help to get him up. He could not hide his physical pain but he never seemed to be depressed. I wanted to face the inevitable openly together.

One day while I was cleaning up the bathroom and he was back in his transport chair, he asked, "How long do we have?" That was the opening for which I had been prayerfully waiting.

I responded, "Do you mean how long do you have to live?" He said, "Yes." I immediately quit what I was doing, put down the lid of his portable potty chair and sat knee to knee, directly facing him. "None of us knows, Stan, but there's something I want you to know. I want to hold your hand until you see an angel, your mother, Jesus, or anyone else who has already died offering a hand to welcome you home. Then I want you to let go of my hand and walk on with them." I added, "It pains me to see you in pain, and for that reason I can accept death."

I felt very much at peace having this conversation with him. I talked earnestly on. "Death will be a good thing for you, Stan. I am the one who will hurt when you die." With tears in my eyes, I added, "I'll be okay though. I truly appreciate all you have done to see that I am settled here and financially secure. I'm not stupid and I'll figure things out as I need to." Tears were welling in his eyes and he lovingly reached out his arms in an effort to embrace and comfort me.

When I regained my composure, I added: "I have no way of knowing what life after death is like, but I do believe in God's grace. It's not how good we have been that is important, but how good God is." It was a precious time for us – emotionally facing the impending future together.

I had very willingly cancelled all of my calendar appointments when we signed on for hospice care and I brought him home. For two months, the hospice nurse came every morning to help get him up, showered and dressed while I got breakfast.

My prayer every night was still one of gratitude for the 61 years we'd had together and my prayer both night and morning was that I'd be given the strength and wisdom to be the very best loving wife I could possibly be as I cared for him. I saw it as a privilege to see him through to the end. "'Till death us do part" was a cherished promise made those 61 years earlier.

I knew he wanted to spend his last days here at home, but again Kim, Jeff, the hospice nurse, hospice social worker, and I realized that I could no longer manage him alone. He was too weak to move even with help from his transport chair to wherever he needed to be. Because of back pain that narcotics couldn't seem to cover, the fact that his skin would tear with the slightest pressure, and even though he was just skin and bones, it took three people to move him.

The realization that I now needed but couldn't have two other people here 24/7 and the fact that Stan had to have more care created a crisis. The social worker called Mennonite Memorial Home that very afternoon to see if there was a room available for him either on the main campus or at Willow Ridge across the road. They said there wasn't.

The next morning, they called to say that Harvey Bauman was willing to share his room. We both knew this long-time member of First Mennonite Church. His wife had died a very few weeks before. We knew he'd make a really good roommate. What providence! That same day, Friday, October 23rd, Stan was admitted to nursing care at Mennonite Memorial Home.

I was grateful that there was only about a mile between us –making it very easy for me to eat lunch with him every day, come home for a nap when he napped, and return to help him with supper in the evenings. We would then watch TV together until his early bedtime.

Friday evening, the 30th of October 2015 was Trick or Treat night at MMH. I talked Stan into sitting in his wheelchair just outside the room where we could hand out candies to hordes of costumed community children including three of our great-grandchildren. Kristen, one of our granddaughters, got a good photo of Stan responding to Leah who was dressed as a little princess. Though we didn't know at the time, it was to be the last photo we'd have of Stan.

I spent the nights of November 6 and 7 (Friday and Saturday nights) at MMH trying to sleep in the uncomfortable recliner beside Stan's bed. Family members stopped in off and on during the weekend even though Stan could not participate much in our conversations. Jeff and his wife said what was their final goodbye to Stan around 3:30 on Sunday, November 8, and headed back to Indiana.

It was around 7:30 when Kim and her family were getting ready to leave. I was sitting on the arm of the recliner holding a cool compress to Stan's forehead with my right hand. With my left hand I was caressing the backs of Stan's hands which were folded on his skinny belly. Suddenly Stan's eyes that had been at half-mast opened wide and focused on the ceiling with a look of amazement. The nurse who had just given him a short of morphine, was standing on the opposite side of his bed. She said, "I think he's seeing things that we don't see."

I thought so too. Stan and I had read and been intrigued by the book and we'd seen the movie of *Heaven Is for Real.* We'd read other such stories in *Guideposts* magazine as well.

I drew close to his ear and spoke softly, "Can you tell me what you are seeing?" He had not spoken all day and he didn't answer. Soft recorded music in the background was playing "How Great Thou Art" –a hymn that he had previously chosen as one he wanted sung at his memorial service.

Moments later, he turned over his right hand and firmly took hold of my left hand. I wondered if that was his way of saying goodbye and I checked to see if his intermittent breathing had stopped. His eyes were still wide open with that look of amazement, but his mouth had peacefully relaxed.

He was gone.

Questions for Individual Reflection and or Group Sharing:

1. As you have thought about your own faith journey, have you recognized more of God's presence and providence in your life? Have you thanked God?

2. Have you thanked family and friends for faith-sharing that has inspired you to new experiences of communication with them and with God in prayer?

3. Are you listening for God's guidance in current circumstances? Regardless of your age, have you written a will and completed medical directive forms?

4. What challenges face you today or in the immediate months or years ahead? Can you trust God to lead and provide?

Addendum:

This Christmas letter to friends and family was written just a little more than a month after Stan died. I include it here because it speaks of my sense of and dependence upon God's presence as together we walked through and beyond the darkness of so many losses.

Greetings to One and All:
Christmas 2015

I hope your days are sunny and bright. The weather has been quite nice here in Bluffton even though Stan and I walked a number of months this year through "the valley of the shadow of death." Psalm 23 was right. We did not walk alone. God's promised presence was very real and I am so grateful for that as well as for the 61 years Stan and I walked hand in hand honoring the promise we made to love and care for each other "till death us do part." The situation was quite un-loveable, but God gave us strength and courage for each day as Stan grew weaker and thinner until he could no longer function. We experienced the different, deeper, and perhaps more divine love that grows through commitment and challenging times. We were surrounded and supported by family and friends as well as Hospice care beginning two months before he died on November 8. He had diminished from his usual 175 to less than 118 pounds --just skin and bones.

Stan had scheduled another vacation for the end of May in Florida where we'd spent two very pleasant weeks a couple of years ago, but we had to cancel that and he spent that time in the hospital instead. Things were different from then on. Our annual family retreat at Quaker Haven had to be cancelled as well. Friends filled in for me as I took what I called a "sabbatical" from all of my responsibilities and usual activities in church and community in order to be available for Stan. Though of course I miss him, his death was truly a blessing. I was intent on being with him when he died. I could describe it more fully, but let it suffice to say that he firmly took my hand. His eyes opened wide in a look of utter amazement toward the ceiling. I softly asked him if he could tell me what he was seeing, but he hadn't spoken all day and he didn't answer. There was just a countenance of peace.

I am slowly getting back into a more typical schedule–beginning with water aerobics. I'm learning a lot about estates, trusts, taxes, etc. with wonderful help from the financial planner that Stan trained and to whom he sold his business. Here's what he wrote to me as we began to sort out all these things that I now need to understand. "Stan certainly gave me many opportunities in life, and I want to show my appreciation by helping you any way I can. You are a valued client, as was Stan, and I look forward to assisting you in the years to come."

I am enjoying the Christmas letters and cards that are coming in. Kim's family celebrated together on the 20th when we could all get together. And on the 25th I'll be with her son Ben and his family in Perrysburg. Jeff and Nancy were terrific in helping me get ready for the memorial service. They are now awaiting the birth of their fifth grandchild and are packed and waiting for the call to go help with their daughter and family when the baby boy decides to greet the world. How I wish the world were a more peaceful and welcoming place.

With Thomas Merton, "When I pray for peace, I pray not only that the enemies of my own country may cease to want war, but above all that my own country will cease to do the things that make war inevitable." I am comforted knowing that faith in our God of Love and Grace provides us a personal peace that takes away fear including the fear of death.

Much love to all,

Ruth Naylor

Acknowledgements

I offer heartfelt thanks to the editors who over the years have chosen the following poems to first appear in their publications, and to the Ohio Poetry Day and LeadingAge judges who selected winners in contests listed below:

"Caught in Communication" - *Christian Living*

"Perspective" - *Catholic Home Messenger, With,* and *The Gem*

"Prayer for Life" – *Progress, Rejoice, With* and *The Gem*

"Delayed Testimony" - *Upon Waking: 58 Voices Speak Out From the Shadows*

"Christmas 1969" – *The Mennonite;* republished as "Blue Christmas" in *Straw & All: A Christmas Poetry Collection*

"This Is Forever" - A *Family Affair*

"(UN)CERTAINTY" - *The Mennonite* and *Evangel*

"Hopeless Hope" – *Socrates Magazine*

"The Storm" - The *Centaur: An Interterm Journal of Opinion*

"A Teacher's Prayer" – *Teachers of Vision*

"Trying" - *The Mennonite* and *Teachers of Vision*

"Time's Twisted Frame" - *With*

"Back to the Basics" - *With*

"Impromptu Reward" - *Straw & All: A Christmas Poetry Collection*

"To Quercus alba and Diospyros ebenum" - *Friendly Woman*

"Two Teachers" - *The Mennonite, Purpose,* and *Findlay Schools Bulletin*

"Facing a Mid-Life Change" – *Purpose, MCC Women's Concerns,* and *Friendly Woman*

"But to Minister?" – *The Mennonite*

"A Prayer" - *Sharing*

"The Circus Performer's Prayer" – *Best of 2008 – Ohio Poetry Day* and *Teachers of Vision*

"Murky Reflection" – *Presence: An International Journal of Spiritual Direction*

"Ella's Easter Morning" - *Christian Living*

"Time for Vacation" - *Christian Living*

"Document This" - *LeadingAge Ohio Contest – 3rd in District, 3rd at State*

"Pre-Planning" - *Best of 2002 – Ohio Poetry Day, Purpose*

"Abstraction" – *Best of 2005 – Ohio Poetry Day*

"Prayer of a Contemporary Pilgrim"--First commissioned by Faith & Life Press for use on a Thanksgiving bulletin cover, then later published in *The Mennonite, Quaker Life, and The Senior Beacon*

I am grateful to the late Lillian Steiner who first suggested that I should put my thoughts on prayer into a book and to the two of my grandchildren, Karen and Ben McCullough, who on that Christmas Day in 2015, coaxed me into telling them how faith has impacted my life --then when dinner was ready long before the stories were finished, said that I must finish my nearly abandoned manuscript for the benefit of all my grandchildren –and others.

I am deeply grateful as well to Joanne Niswander who graciously gave of her time and editorial expertise reading my manuscript carefully, catching errors and suggesting places where more explanation either in prose or poetry might clarify certain sections. I offer my thanks to her and the rest of the Bluffton Writers who kept me working on this memoir over a period of many years.

Sheri Lynn Robertson went out of her way at a recent family wedding to take the "author photo" for this book. Thank you, Sheri.

And this list of acknowledgements would not be complete without also thanking the many professional staff members at WestBow Publishing for their assistance in making this spiritual memoir widely available.

Prayer of a Contemporary Pilgrim

Thank you, God,

For all the obvious things

For all the things we forget
to remember

And for all the things
we'd just as soon forget.

About the Author

Ruth E. Bundy Naylor was raised in a Conservative Quaker community and attended public school at Mt. Pleasant, OH, prior to receiving four years of high school education at Olney Friends Boarding School in Barnesville, OH. She earned a B.A. from Bluffton College (now Bluffton University) and the M.A. degree from Bowling Green State University. She later studied at Associated Mennonite Biblical Seminary in Elkhart, IN, received clinical pastoral education at Lutheran Hospital in Ft. Wayne, IN, and completed a two-year course in spiritual guidance from Shalem Institute in Washington, D.C. She regularly attends Writers' Colloquiums and Spirituality Workshops at Earlham School of Religion in Richmond, IN.

Early work experience included being stenographer for the Superintendent and Assistant Superintendent at Methodist Hospital in Indianapolis, IN., and Administrative Assistant to the Vice President in charge of a life insurance company's home office in Ft. Wayne, IN. The next ten years were devoted to motherhood, happy homemaking, creative writing, helping to plant a church, and then completing work for her B.A. when the children were both in school.

Ruth was a substitute teacher for one year and then taught in the English Department at Bluffton High School for twelve years, during which time she was active in General Conference Mennonite Church district and national committees.

Subsequently she was invited to join the pastoral staff at her local church where she was later ordained and served for twelve years prior to serving as Interim Conference Minister for the Central District. She served on the Integration Exploration Committee of the General Conference and the Mennonite Church and then on the national board of Mennonite Church USA and on the Joint Executive Committee of MCUSA and Mennonite Church Canada.

In retirement, she has continued as an ecumenical spiritual director for individual pastors and interested lay persons. She has continued her interest in writing –teaching courses in the Bluffton University Institute for Learning in Retirement and chairing the Bluffton Writers' Group. Well over 100 of her poems and articles have appeared in a wide variety of Christian publications. She has also published two collections of poetry.

Ruth and her late husband, Stan, gave birth to a daughter, Kimberly Anne McCullough, and a son, Geoffrey Alan Naylor. The family now includes seven grandchildren and thirteen great-grandchildren.

Ruth can be reached at renaylor34@gmail.com